WONDERFUL
ONE-POTS

D1345039

WONDERFUL ONE-POTS

COLLINS & BROWN

The Good Housekeeping website is
www.goodhousekeeping.co.uk

ISBN 978-1-909397-54-5

A catalogue record for this book is available from
the British Library.

Reproduction by Mission Productions Ltd, Hong
Kong
Printed and bound by 1010 Printing International Ltd,
China

This book can be ordered direct from the publisher.
Contact the marketing department, but try your
bookshop first.

www.anovabooks.com

NOTES

Both metric and imperial measures are given for
the recipes. Follow either set of measures, not a
mixture of both, as they are not interchangeable.

All spoon measures are level.
1 tsp = 5ml spoon; 1 tbsp = 15ml spoon.

Ovens and grills must be preheated to the specified
temperature.

Medium eggs should be used except where
otherwise specified. Free-range eggs are
recommended.

Note that some recipes contain raw or lightly
cooked eggs. The young, elderly, pregnant women
and anyone with an immune-deficiency disease
should avoid these because of the slight risk of
salmonella.

Contents

Midweek Suppers

Throw-it-all-together Salad

Hands-on time: 10 minutes

2–4 chargrilled chicken breasts,
   torn into strips
2 carrots, peeled into strips
½ cucumber, halved lengthways,
   seeded and cut into ribbons
a handful of fresh coriander leaves,
   roughly chopped
½ head of Chinese leaves, shredded
4 handfuls of watercress
4 spring onions, shredded

For the dressing
5 tbsp peanut butter
2 tbsp sweet chilli sauce
juice of 1 lime
salt and freshly ground black pepper

1 Put all the salad ingredients into a large salad bowl.
2 To make the dressing, put the peanut butter, chilli sauce and lime juice in a small bowl and mix together well. Season with salt and pepper. Add 2–3 tbsp cold water, a tablespoon at a time, to thin the dressing if it's too thick to pour. Use just enough water to make the dressing the right consistency.
3 Drizzle the dressing over the salad, toss together and serve.

Serves 4

Spiced Beef and Noodle Soup

Hands-on time: 20 minutes, plus soaking
Cooking time: 15 minutes

2 tbsp sunflower oil

225g (8oz) fillet steak, cut into
thin strips

1.1 litres (2 pints) beef stock

2–3 tbsp Thai fish sauce (nam pla)

1 large red chilli, seeded and finely
sliced

1 lemongrass stalk, trimmed and
thinly sliced

2.5cm (1in) piece of root ginger, peeled
and finely shredded

6 spring onions, halved lengthways
and cut into 2.5cm (1in) lengths

1 garlic clove, crushed

¼ tsp caster sugar

15g (½oz) dried porcini or shiitake
mushrooms, broken into pieces and
soaked in 150ml (¼ pint) boiling
water for 15 minutes

50g (2oz) medium egg noodles

125g (4oz) spinach leaves,
roughly chopped

4 tbsp freshly chopped coriander

salt and freshly ground black pepper

1 Heat the oil in a large pan, then
brown the meat in two batches and
put to one side.

2 Pour the stock into the pan
with 2 tbsp of the fish sauce, the
chilli, lemongrass, ginger, spring
onions, garlic and sugar. Add the
mushrooms and their soaking
liquid. Bring the mixture to the boil.

3 Break up the noodles slightly and
add them to the pan, then stir gently
until they begin to separate. Simmer
the soup, stirring occasionally, for
4–5 minutes until the noodles are
just tender.

4 Stir in the spinach, coriander and
reserved beef. Season with salt and
ground black pepper, adding the
remaining fish sauce to taste, then
serve the soup in warmed bowls.

Serves 4

Smoked Cod and Sweetcorn Chowder

Hands-on time: 20 minutes
Cooking time: 20 minutes

130g pack cubed pancetta

50g (2oz) butter

3 leeks, about 450g (1lb), trimmed and thinly sliced

25g (1oz) plain flour

600ml (1 pint) semi-skimmed or full-fat milk

700g (1½lb) undyed smoked cod loin or haddock, skinned and cut into 2cm (¾in) cubes

326g can sweetcorn in water, drained

450g (1lb) small new potatoes, sliced

150ml (¼ pint) double cream

½ tsp paprika

salt and freshly ground black pepper

2 tbsp freshly chopped flat-leafed parsley to garnish

1 Fry the pancetta in a large pan over a gentle heat until the fat runs out. Add the butter to the pan to melt, then add the leeks and cook until softened.

2 Stir in the flour and cook for a few seconds, then pour in the milk and 300ml (½ pint) cold water. Add the fish to the pan with the sweetcorn and potatoes. Bring to the boil, then reduce the heat and simmer for 10–15 minutes until the potatoes are cooked.

3 Stir in the cream, season with salt and ground black pepper and the paprika, and cook for 2–3 minutes to warm through. Ladle into warmed shallow bowls and sprinkle each one with a little chopped parsley. Serve immediately.

Serves 6

Goulash in a Hurry

Hands-on time: 20 minutes
Cooking time: 20 minutes

½ tbsp olive oil

1 onion, finely sliced

500g (1lb 2oz) lean pork steaks, cut into finger-sized strips

50ml (2fl oz) dry vermouth (optional)

1 tbsp paprika

1 tbsp plain flour

2 tbsp tomato purée

2 × 400g cans chopped tomatoes

2 red peppers, deseeded and cut into strips

salt and freshly ground black pepper

a small handful of fresh coriander, chopped, to garnish

low-fat Greek yogurt to dollop

boiled rice to serve

1 Heat the oil in a large pan, add the onion and fry for 10 minutes, until lightly coloured. Add the pork strips and fry for 5 minutes. Carefully pour in the vermouth, if using, then stir in the paprika, flour and tomato purée and cook for 1 minute.

2 Add the tomatoes, peppers, a splash of water and some seasoning, and simmer, stirring occasionally, for 5 minutes.

3 Check the seasoning and garnish with coriander and a dollop of yogurt. Serve with rice.

Serves 4

Zingy Fish

Hands-on time: about 10 minutes
Cooking time: 12 minutes

125g (4oz) tenderstem broccoli, halved lengthways

250g (9oz) fine asparagus

4 × 125g (4oz) skinless and boneless white fish fillets, such as haddock, pollock, cod or coley, ideally sustainably caught

50ml (2fl oz) white wine

1 orange, cut into 8 wedges

75g (3oz) sourdough bread, torn into pieces

2 tbsp olive oil

salt and freshly ground black pepper

boiled rice or salad to serve

1 Preheat the oven to 220°C (200°C fan) mark 7. Spread the broccoli and asparagus in an even layer in a medium roasting tin. Lay the fish fillets on top and pour over the wine. Tuck the orange wedges and bread around the fish. Drizzle over the olive oil and season well.

2 Cook in the oven for 10–12 minutes, or until the fish is cooked through and the vegetables are just tender (they should still have bite). Serve immediately with some boiled rice or salad.

Serves 4

Perfect Wok

You don't need to buy special equipment to start stir-frying – a large deep-sided frying pan and a spatula will do the job – but a wok is very versatile, with many uses in the kitchen.

Choosing a wok

Traditional steel woks have rounded bottoms, so the food always returns to the centre where the heat is most intense. The deep sides prevent the food from falling out during stir-frying. Most woks now have flattened bottoms, which makes them more stable on modern hobs. Non-stick woks are widely available; they are easy to clean and not prone to rusting.

- There are two main styles of wok, one with double handles opposite each other, the other with one long handle. The double-handled wok gets very hot and needs to be handled with oven gloves, although it is slightly more stable if you use it for steaming and braising. A wok with a long single handle is the best choice as it is easier to manipulate when stir-frying.
- A wok with a diameter of 35.5cm (14in) is most useful for cooking stir-fries for four people.
- A well-fitting lid is useful if you intend to use your wok for steaming.

Wok equipment

Wok spoon A metal utensil with a curved end to match the curve of the wok is useful for stir-frying in a traditional steel wok, but should not be used in non-stick woks – any heatproof spatula will do.

Chopsticks Long wooden chopsticks are great for stir-frying in non-stick woks; they are also useful for separating blocks of noodles as they cook.

Steamers These come in various sizes, and may be of pierced metal or bamboo. They can be used in a wok or over a pan of boiling water, covered with a tight-fitting lid.

Trivet or steamer rack A wooden or metal trivet or steamer rack fits inside the wok to keep food above the water level when steaming.

Wok stand A wok stand or ring, which sits on the hob with the wok on top, helps keep the wok stable during steaming or braising.

Strainer A long-handled strainer is useful for scooping food from deep-frying oil, but a slotted spoon could be used instead.

Seasoning a wok

Non-stick woks do not need to be seasoned. Traditional steel woks, designed to withstand high temperatures, can be made practically non-stick by 'seasoning' before you use them for the first time. First scrub the wok in hot water and detergent, then dry thoroughly with kitchen paper. Place it over a low heat, add 2 tbsp groundnut oil and rub this over the entire inner surface with kitchen paper. Keep the wok over a low heat until the oil starts to smoke. Leave to cool for 5 minutes, then rub well with kitchen paper. Add another 2 tbsp oil and repeat the heating process twice more until the kitchen paper wipes clean. The wok is now seasoned. If used regularly it should remain rust-free. After each use, rinse in hot water – but not detergent – and wipe clean with kitchen paper. If you scrub your wok or use detergent you will need to season it again.

Stir-frying Vegetables

Stir-frying is perfect for non-starchy vegetables, as the quick cooking preserves their colour, freshness and texture.

Perfect stir-frying

- Cut everything into small pieces of uniform size so that they cook quickly and evenly.
- If you're cooking onions or garlic with the vegetables, don't keep them in the high heat for too long or they will burn.
- Add liquids towards the end of cooking so they don't evaporate.

You will need: 450g (1lb) vegetables, 1–2 tbsp vegetable oil, 2 crushed garlic cloves, 2 tbsp soy sauce, 2 tsp sesame oil.

1. Cut the vegetables into even-size pieces. Heat the oil in a large wok or frying pan until smoking-hot. Add the garlic and cook for a few seconds, then remove and put to one side.

2. Add the vegetables to the wok, then toss and stir them. Keep them moving constantly as they cook, which will take 4–5 minutes.

3. When the vegetables are just tender, but still with a slight bite, turn off the heat. Put the garlic back into the wok and stir well. Add the soy sauce and sesame oil, toss and serve.

Chilli Vegetable and Coconut Stir-fry

🍴 **Hands-on time:** 25 minutes
Cooking time: about 10 minutes

2 tbsp sesame oil

2 green chillies, seeded and finely chopped

2.5cm (1in) piece of fresh root ginger, peeled and finely grated

2 garlic cloves, crushed

1 tbsp Thai green curry paste

125g (4oz) carrot, cut into fine matchsticks

125g (4oz) baby sweetcorn, halved

125g (4oz) mangetouts, halved on the diagonal

2 large red peppers, finely sliced

2 small pak choi, quartered

4 spring onions, finely chopped

300ml (½ pint) coconut milk

2 tbsp peanut satay sauce

2 tbsp light soy sauce

1 tsp soft brown sugar

4 tbsp freshly chopped coriander, plus extra sprigs to garnish

freshly ground black pepper

roasted peanuts to garnish

boiled rice or noodles to serve

1 Heat the oil in a wok or large non-stick frying pan over a medium heat. Add the chillies, ginger and garlic and stir-fry for 1 minute. Add the curry paste and fry for a further 30 seconds.

2 Add the carrot, sweetcorn, mangetouts and red peppers. Stir-fry over a high heat for 3–4 minutes, then add the pak choi and spring onions. Cook, stirring, for a further 1–2 minutes.

3 Pour in the coconut milk, satay sauce, soy sauce and sugar. Season with pepper, bring to the boil and cook for 1–2 minutes, then add the chopped coriander. Garnish with the peanuts and coriander sprigs, and serve with rice or noodles.

Serves 4

Pea, Mint and Ricotta Pasta

Hands-on time: 5 minutes
Cooking time: 10 minutes

300g (11oz) farfalle pasta
200g (7oz) frozen peas
175g (6oz) vegetarian ricotta
3 tbsp freshly chopped mint
2 tbsp extra virgin olive oil
salt and freshly ground black pepper

1 Cook the pasta according to the pack instructions. Add the frozen peas for the last 4 minutes of cooking.

2 Drain the pasta and peas, keeping the water to one side, then put back into the pan. Stir in the ricotta and mint with a ladleful of the cooking water. Season well, drizzle with the oil and serve at once.

Serves 4

Classic Eggs

Follow these tried and tested steps for perfect baked eggs and omelettes.

Baking

You can crack eggs into individual dishes or into a large shallow pan and bake them. They may be cooked on their own, or baked with vegetable accompaniments.

1 Generously smear individual baking dishes or one large baking dish with butter.

2 Put in any accompaniments, if using (see Variations and accompaniments, opposite). If using vegetable-based accompaniments, use the back of a spoon to make a hollow in which to carefully break each egg.

3 Bake for 8–10 minutes at 200°C (180°C fan oven) mark 6, or 15–18 minutes at 180°C (160°C fan oven) mark 4 until the whites are set; the yolks should still be quite runny.

Variations and accompaniments

Eggs are delicious baked on a simple bed of sautéed vegetables (such as ratatouille), lightly browned diced potatoes with onions, and also on some well-cooked spinach. Accompaniments must be fully cooked before they are transferred to the dish and the raw eggs put on top. Other simple additions include freshly chopped herbs. If you like, drizzle a small spoonful of cream and a good grinding of black pepper on top of the eggs before baking.

Perfect omelettes

- ❏ Don't add butter until the pan is already hot, otherwise it will brown too much
- ❏ Beat the eggs lightly
- ❏ Use a high heat

Classic omelette

1 To make an omelette for one person, heat a heavy-based 18cm (7in) frying pan or omelette pan. Using a fork, beat 2 eggs and season with salt and freshly ground black pepper.

2 Add 15g (½oz) butter to the pan and let it sizzle for a few moments without browning, then pour in the eggs and stir a few times with a fork.

3 As the omelette begins to stick at the sides, lift it up and allow the uncooked egg to run into the gap.

4 When the omelette is nearly set and the underneath is brown, loosen the edges and give the pan a sharp shake to slide the omelette across.

5 Add a filling (such as grated cheese or fried mushrooms), if you like, and fold the far side of the omelette towards you. Tilt the pan to slide the omelette on to the plate and serve.

Huevos Rancheros

Hands-on time: 10 minutes
Cooking time: about 15 minutes

1 tbsp vegetable oil,
1 medium red onion, finely sliced
1 each yellow and red pepper, seeded
    and finely sliced
1 red chilli, seeded and finely sliced
2 × 400g cans chopped tomatoes
½ tsp dried mixed herbs
4 large eggs
salt and freshly ground black pepper
a small handful of fresh flat-leafed
    parsley, roughly chopped, to garnish
crusty bread, to serve

1 Heat the oil in a large frying pan over a high heat. Add the onion, peppers and chilli and fry for 3 minutes until just softened. Add the tomatoes and dried herbs. Season with salt and ground black pepper and simmer for 3 minutes.

2 Break an egg into a small cup. Use a wooden spoon to scrape a hole in the tomato mixture, then quickly drop in the egg. Repeat with the remaining eggs, spacing evenly around the tomato mixture. Cover and simmer for 3–5 minutes until the eggs are just set. Sprinkle with parsley and serve with crusty bread.

Serves 6

Gruyère and Watercress Omelette

Hands-on time: 5 minutes
Cooking time: 5 minutes

½ tbsp vegetable oil
2–3 seasoned and lightly beaten large eggs
a small handful of watercress, roughly chopped
25g (1oz) grated Gruyère cheese
green salad and crusty bread to serve

1 Heat the oil in a small frying pan over a low heat. Add 2–3 eggs (depending on hunger!) and use a spatula to move them around the pan for the first 30 seconds.
2 Next, top the egg with the watercress and grated Gruyère cheese.
3 Continue cooking until the base of the omelette is golden (check with the spatula) and the cheese is melting. Fold in half and serve with a green salad and crusty bread.

Serves 1

Slow and Steady

Perfect Poultry, Meat and Game

Most poultry and game birds from the butcher or supermarket are sold already plucked, drawn and ready for the oven. Look for birds with no signs of damage or blemishes. If the birds are not wrapped in plastic, check that they smell pleasant. Generally, the larger the bird, the greater proportion of meat to bone there will be – and therefore better value. Check that the birds have a neat shape, an even colour and no bruises or tears on the skin. The body should look meaty and plump. Some whole birds are bought with a packet of giblets (neck, liver, heart and crop) tucked inside the carcass. Remove and store them in a sealed container in the fridge, to use within a day. Put the bird in a shallow dish, cover with clingfilm and store in the fridge. Use within two days, or according to the 'use-by' date on its label. Poultry from the supermarket can be left in its original packaging.

Where possible, when you are buying poultry and game birds, try to support your local butcher. You will be rewarded with great produce and choice.

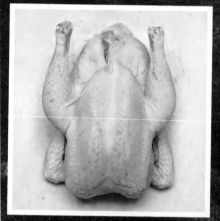

How to buy and store meat and game

Each animal can be divided into different cuts, all of which have their own characteristic flavour and texture. Cuts from parts of the animal that have worked hardest, for example the shin or neck, contain the toughest muscle tissue and usually require long, slow cooking. Cuts from parts that have worked the least, like the fore-rib or sirloin, are more tender and suit quicker cooking. It's important to choose the right cut when buying meat for a recipe – if you want beef for a speedy stir-fry, for example, you will need a tender, quick-cooking cut such as sirloin.

When buying meat and game, always check it first: it should look and smell fresh. The flesh should look moist but not watery, and pink, red or dark red according to variety (mature beef will be dark red, as will venison). Fat should be pale, creamy and firm – avoid meat where the fat is crumbly, waxy or yellowing. Look for meat that has been well cut and trimmed and remember that some fat will add flavour.

Meat should be wrapped and stored in the fridge, placed in a dish so that if any juices escape they cannot drip and contaminate other foods. Do not allow the meat to touch any other foods. Raw meat can generally be stored for three to five days, although offal and minced or processed meat such as sausages can deteriorate more quickly and should be used within two days. Meat that is bought sealed in a pack can be stored in the fridge unopened, making sure that it is eaten before the use-by date.

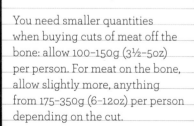

You need smaller quantities when buying cuts of meat off the bone: allow 100–150g (3½–5oz) per person. For meat on the bone, allow slightly more, anything from 175–350g (6–12oz) per person depending on the cut.

How to Joint a Chicken

You can buy pieces of chicken in a supermarket or from a butcher, but it is more economical to joint a whole bird yourself.

1 Using a sharp meat knife with a curved blade, cut out the wishbone and remove the wings in a single piece. Remove the wing tips.

2 With the tail pointing towards you and breast side up, pull one leg away from the body and cut through the skin between the leg and breast. Pull the leg down until you crack the joint between the thigh bone and rib cage. Cut through that joint, then cut through the remaining leg meat. Repeat on the other side.

3 To remove the breast without any bone, make a cut along the length of the breastbone. Gently teasing the flesh away from the ribs with the knife, work the blade down between the flesh and ribs of one breast and cut it off neatly. (Always cut in,

towards the bone.) Repeat on the other side.

4 To remove the breast with the bone in, make a cut along the full length of the breastbone. Using poultry shears, cut through the breastbone, then cut through the rib cage following the outline of the breast meat. Repeat on the other side. Trim off any flaps of skin or fat.

Perfect Casseroling

There are a number of ways to make the most of the delicate taste of poultry. Here's how to make the perfect casserole.

Chicken Casserole

To serve 4–6, you will need:
1 jointed chicken, 3 tbsp oil, 1 chopped onion, 2 crushed garlic cloves, 2 chopped celery sticks, 2 chopped carrots, 1 tbsp plain flour, 2 tbsp freshly chopped tarragon or thyme, chicken stock and/or wine, salt and freshly ground black pepper.

1 Preheat the oven to 180°C (160°C fan oven) mark 4. Cut the chicken legs and breasts in half.

2 Heat the oil in a flameproof casserole and brown the chicken all over. Remove the chicken and pour off the excess oil. Add the onion and garlic and brown for a few minutes. Add the vegetables, then stir in the flour and cook for 1 minute. Add the herbs and season. Add the chicken and pour in the stock and/or wine to come three-quarters of the way up the poultry. Bring to the boil, then cover and cook in the oven for 1–1½ hours.

Chicken and Vegetable Pot

Hands-on time: 20 minutes
Cooking time: 1 hour 40 minutes

2 tbsp olive oil

1 large onion, cut into wedges

2 rindless streaky bacon rashers, chopped

1 chicken, about 1.6kg (3½lb)

6 carrots

2 small turnips, cut into wedges

1 garlic clove, crushed

bouquet garni (1 bay leaf, a few fresh parsley and thyme sprigs)

600ml (1 pint) hot chicken stock

100ml (3½fl oz) dry white wine

12 button mushrooms

3 tbsp freshly chopped flat-leafed parsley

salt and freshly ground black pepper

mashed potatoes to serve (optional)

1 Heat the oil in a non-stick flameproof casserole. Add the onion and bacon and fry for 5 minutes or until golden. Remove and put to one side.

2 Add the whole chicken to the casserole and fry for 10 minutes, turning carefully to brown all over. Remove and put to one side.

3 Preheat the oven to 200°C (180°C fan oven) mark 6. Add the carrots, turnips and garlic to the casserole and fry for 5 minutes, then add the onion and bacon. Put the chicken back into the casserole, add the bouquet garni, hot stock, wine and seasoning. Bring to a simmer, cover and cook in the oven for 30 minutes.

4 Remove the casserole from the oven and add the mushrooms. Baste the chicken, then re-cover and cook for a further 50 minutes.

5 Lift out the chicken, then stir the parsley into the cooking liquid. Carve the chicken and serve with the vegetables and cooking liquid, and mashed potatoes, if you like.

Serves 6

Pork and Apple Hotpot

Hands-on time: 15 minutes
Cooking time: about 2¼ hours

1 tbsp olive oil

900g (2lb) pork shoulder steaks

3 onions, cut into wedges

1 large Bramley apple, peeled, cored
  and thickly sliced

1 tbsp plain flour

600ml (1 pint) hot weak vegetable
  or chicken stock

¼ Savoy cabbage, sliced

2 fresh thyme sprigs

900g (2lb) large potatoes, cut into
  2cm (¾in) slices

25g (1oz) butter

salt and freshly ground black pepper

1 Preheat the oven to 170°C (150°C fan oven) mark 3. Heat the oil in a large non-stick flameproof casserole until very hot, then fry the steaks, two at a time, for 5 minutes or until golden all over. Remove the steaks from the pan and put to one side.

2 In the same casserole, fry the onions for 10 minutes or until soft – add a little water if they start to stick. Stir in the apple and cook for 1 minute, then add the flour to soak up the juices. Gradually add the hot stock and stir until smooth. Season, then

FREEZE AHEAD

To make ahead and freeze, use a freezerproof casserole. Complete the recipe, cool quickly, then freeze in the casserole for up to three months. To use, thaw overnight at cool room temperature. Preheat the oven to 180°C (160°C fan oven) mark 4. Pour 50ml (2fl oz) hot stock over the hotpot, then cover and reheat for 30 minutes or until piping hot. Uncover and crisp the potatoes under the grill for 2–3 minutes.

stir in the cabbage and add the pork. Throw in the thyme, overlap the potato slices on top, then dot with the butter.

3 Cover with a tight-fitting lid and cook near the top of the oven for 1 hour. Remove the lid and cook for 30–45 minutes until the potatoes are tender and golden. Put the hotpot under the grill for 2–3 minutes to crisp up the potatoes, if you like.

Scotch Broth

Hands-on time: 15 minutes
Cooking time: about 1 hour

1 tbsp vegetable oil
250g (9oz) lamb neck fillets, cut into
  2cm (¾in) cubes
2 parsnips, roughly chopped
2 carrots, roughly chopped
1 onion, finely chopped
1 potato, finely diced
3 smoked streaky bacon rashers,
  finely sliced
125g (4oz) pearl barley
1 litre (1¾ pints) lamb stock
75g (3oz) frozen peas
salt and freshly ground black pepper
a small handful of fresh parsley,
  finely chopped, to garnish

1 Heat the oil over a high heat in a large casserole. Brown the lamb all over – do this in batches if necessary to stop the lamb from sweating rather than browning. Add the parsnips, carrots, onion, potato and bacon and fry for 3-5 minutes.

2 Add the pearl barley and mix well. Pour in the stock and stir well, scraping any sticky goodness from the bottom of the casserole. Bring to the boil, then reduce the heat, cover and simmer gently for 40-50 minutes until the lamb is tender.

3 Stir in the peas, heat through, then check the seasoning. Transfer to individual bowls, garnish the broth with parsley and serve.

Serves 4

Lamb and Orzo Stew

Hands-on time: 10 minutes
Cooking time: about 2 hours

1 tbsp vegetable oil

1kg (2¼lb) diced lamb (leg or shoulder), excess fat trimmed

2 red onions, finely sliced

1 tbsp dried oregano

1 tsp ground cinnamon

400g can chopped tomatoes

1.2 litres (2¼ pints) vegetable stock

200g (7oz) orzo pasta

50g (2oz) pitted black olives, roughly chopped

a large handful of fresh parsley, roughly chopped

salt and freshly ground black pepper

FREEZE AHEAD

To make ahead and freeze, prepare the stew to the end of step 2, then leave to cool completely. Transfer the mixture to a freezerproof container, cover and freeze for up to three months.

Thaw overnight in the fridge. Reheat gently in a large pan and complete the recipe to serve.

1 Heat the oil in a large heatproof casserole dish or pan and brown the lamb in batches. Once all the meat is browned, lift out and put to one side on a plate.

2 Put the casserole/pan back onto the heat, add the onions and cook gently for 10 minutes or until softened (add a little water if the pan looks too dry). Stir in the oregano and cinnamon and cook for 1 minute, then stir in the tomatoes, stock and lamb. Cover and simmer for 1¼ hours, stirring occasionally, or until the lamb is tender.

3 Stir the orzo into the casserole/pan and cook, uncovered, for a further 10–12 minutes until the orzo is tender. (Once the orzo is tender, it will continue to swell on standing. If you're not serving it immediately, add a little extra water until the desired consistency is reached.) Next, stir in the olives and most of the parsley. Check the seasoning and garnish with the remaining parsley. Serve immediately.

Serves 6

Perfect Braising and Pot-roasting

Tougher cuts require slow cooking. Braises and pot roasts are similar but braises need more liquid.

Tips for perfect results

- ❏ Good cuts of beef include shin, chuck, blade, brisket and flank; good cuts of lamb include leg, shoulder, neck, breast and shank
- ❏ Cuts you would normally roast can also be casseroled. These simply need less time in the oven
- ❏ Always use a low heat and check regularly to make sure that there is enough liquid to keep the meat from catching on the bottom of the casserole
- ❏ Braises often improve by being cooked in advance and then gently reheated before serving. If you've braised a whole piece of meat, you can slice it before reheating

Braised Lamb Shanks

To serve six, you will need:
3 tbsp olive oil, 6 lamb shanks,
1 large onion, 3 carrots, 3 celery
sticks, all thickly sliced, 2 crushed
garlic cloves, 2 × 400g cans
chopped tomatoes, 150ml (¼ pint)
white wine, 2 bay leaves, salt and
freshly ground black pepper.

1 Preheat the oven to 170°C (150°C
   fan oven) mark 3. Heat the oil in
   a large flameproof casserole and
   lightly brown the lamb shanks
   all over, two or three at a time.
   Remove from the pan and put to
   one side. Add the onion, carrots,
   celery and garlic and cook until
   beginning to colour, then add
   the lamb, tomatoes and wine.

2 Stir well, season and add the bay
   leaves. Bring to the boil, then
   cover and transfer to the oven
   for 2 hours or until tender. Skim
   off any fat if necessary.

Braised Lamb Shanks with Cannellini Beans

Hands-on time: 15 minutes
Cooking time: about 2¾ hours

3 tbsp olive oil

6 lamb shanks

1 large onion, chopped

3 carrots, sliced

3 celery sticks, trimmed and sliced

2 garlic cloves, crushed

2 × 400g cans chopped tomatoes

125ml (4fl oz) balsamic vinegar

2 bay leaves

2 × 400g cans cannellini beans,
   drained and rinsed

salt and freshly ground black pepper

1 Preheat the oven to 170°C (150°C fan oven) mark 3. Heat the oil in a large flameproof casserole and brown the lamb shanks, in two batches, all over. Remove and put to one side.

2 Add the onion, carrots, celery and garlic to the casserole and cook gently until softened and just beginning to colour.

3 Put the lamb back into the casserole, add the tomatoes and vinegar and give the mixture a good stir. Season with salt and ground black pepper and add the bay leaves. Bring to a simmer, cover and cook on the hob for 5 minutes.

4 Transfer to the oven and cook for 1½–2 hours until the lamb shanks are nearly tender.

5 Take the casserole out of the oven and add the cannellini beans. Cover and put back into the oven for a further 30 minutes, then serve.

Serves 6

Braised Beef with Pancetta and Mushrooms

🍴 **Hands-on time:** 20 minutes
Cooking time: about 3½ hours

175g (6oz) smoked pancetta or smoked streaky bacon, cubed

2 leeks, trimmed and thickly sliced

1 tbsp olive oil

450g (1lb) braising steak, cut into 5cm (2in) pieces

1 large onion, finely chopped

2 carrots, thickly sliced

2 parsnips, thickly sliced

1 tbsp plain flour

300ml (½ pint) red wine

1–2 tbsp redcurrant jelly

125g (4oz) chestnut mushrooms, halved

freshly ground black pepper

freshly chopped flat-leafed parsley to garnish

1 Preheat the oven to 170°C (150°C fan oven) mark 3. Fry the pancetta or bacon in a shallow flameproof casserole for 2–3 minutes until golden. Add the leeks and cook for a further 2 minutes or until they are just beginning to colour. Remove with a slotted spoon and put to one side.

2 Heat the oil in the casserole. Fry the beef in batches for 2–3 minutes until golden brown on all sides. Remove and put to one side. Add the onion and fry over a gentle heat for 5 minutes or until golden. Stir in the carrots and parsnips and fry for 1–2 minutes.

3 Put the beef back into the casserole and stir in the flour to soak up the juices. Gradually add the wine and 300ml (½ pint) water, then stir in the redcurrant jelly. Season with ground black pepper and bring to the boil. Cover with a tight-fitting lid and cook in the oven for 2 hours.

4 Stir in the leeks, pancetta and mushrooms, cover and cook for a further 1 hour or until everything is tender. Serve hot, sprinkled with chopped parsley.

Serves 4

FREEZE AHEAD
To make ahead and freeze, complete the recipe to the end of step
4, without the garnish. Put into a freezerproof container, cool and
freeze for up to three months. To use, thaw overnight at cool room
temperature. Preheat the oven to 180°C (160°C fan oven) mark
4. Bring the braise to the boil on the hob, then cover tightly and
reheat in the oven for about 30 minutes until piping hot.

Paprika Beef Stew

Hands-on time: 20 minutes
Cooking time: 1¼ hours

1 tbsp sunflower oil

750g (1lb 11oz) braising steak, excess fat trimmed, cut into 2cm (¾in) cubes

25g (1oz) plain flour

1 red onion, roughly chopped

1 each red and green pepper, seeded and roughly chopped

1½ tsp paprika

5 tbsp tomato purée

500ml (17fl oz) beef stock

250g (9oz) long-grain rice

salt and freshly ground black pepper

fresh coriander or parsley to garnish

cream, to drizzle (optional)

1 Heat the oil in a large pan over a medium heat. Meanwhile, dust the beef with the flour, making sure every bit is coated. Brown the beef in the pan (do this in batches if necessary to avoid overcrowding the pan).

2 Once all the beef is browned and put back into the pan, add the onion, peppers, paprika and tomato purée and fry for 5 minutes. Pour in the stock, bring to the boil, then cover, reduce the heat and simmer for 1 hour or until the beef is tender. Take the lid off for the final 15 minutes of the cooking time, stirring occasionally.

3 When the beef has 15 minutes left to cook, boil the rice according to the pack instructions.

4 Check the stew seasoning. Garnish the beef with the coriander or parsley and a drizzle of cream, if you like. Serve with the rice.

FREEZE AHEAD

To make ahead and freeze, prepare to the end of step 2, leave to cool completely, then cover and freeze for up to a month. To serve, defrost thoroughly, gently reheat and complete the recipe to serve.

Serves 4

Peppered Winter Stew

Hands-on time: 20 minutes
Cooking time: about 2¾ hours

25g (1oz) plain flour

900g (2lb) stewing venison, beef or
  lamb, cut into 4cm (1½in) cubes

5 tbsp vegetable or olive oil

225g (8oz) whole button onions
  or shallots

225g (8oz) onion, finely chopped

4 garlic cloves, crushed

2 tbsp tomato purée

125ml (4fl oz) red wine vinegar

750ml bottle red wine

2 tbsp redcurrant jelly

1 small bunch of fresh thyme, plus
  extra sprigs to garnish (optional)

4 bay leaves

6 cloves

900g (2lb) mixed root vegetables, such
  as carrots, parsnips, turnips and
  celeriac, cut into 4cm (1½in) chunks;
  carrots cut a little smaller

600–900ml (1–1½ pints) beef stock

salt and freshly ground black pepper

1 Preheat the oven to 180°C (160°C
  fan oven) mark 4. Put the flour into
  a plastic bag, season with salt and
  ground black pepper, then toss the
  meat in it.

2 Heat 3 tbsp of the oil in a large
  flameproof casserole over a medium
  heat and brown the meat well in
  small batches. Remove and put to
  one side.

3 Heat the remaining oil and fry
  the button onions or shallots
  for 5 minutes or until golden.
  Add the onion and the garlic and
  cook, stirring, until soft and golden.
  Add the tomato purée and cook for
  a further 2 minutes, then add the
  vinegar and wine and bring to
  the boil. Bubble for 10 minutes.

4 Add the redcurrant jelly, thyme, bay
  leaves, 1 tbsp pepper, the cloves and
  meat to the pan, with the vegetables
  and enough stock to barely cover
  the meat and vegetables. Bring
  to the boil, then reduce the heat,
  cover the pan and cook in the oven
  for 1¾–2¼ hours until the meat is
  very tender. Serve hot, garnished
  with thyme sprigs, if you like.

Serves 6

FREEZE AHEAD

To make ahead and freeze, complete the recipe to the end of step 4, without the garnish. Cool quickly and put into a freezerproof container. Seal and freeze for up to one month. To use, thaw overnight at cool room temperature. Preheat the oven to 180°C (160°C fan oven) mark 4. Put the stew into a flameproof casserole, add an extra 150ml (¼ pint) beef stock and bring to the boil. Cover and reheat for 30 minutes.

Haddock and Tomato Casserole

Hands-on time: 15 minutes
Cooking time: about 55 minutes

2 tbsp olive oil

4 shallots, finely chopped

1 leek, finely sliced

2 medium potatoes, about 400g (14oz), cut into 1cm (½in) pieces

150ml (5fl oz) white wine

2 × 400g cans chopped tomatoes

1½ tsp dried oregano

pinch of sugar

4 × 125g (4oz) haddock or other white fish fillets, skinned

salt and fresly ground black pepper

a large handful of fresh basil, roughly chopped, to garnish

1 Heat half the oil in a large flameproof casserole. Add the shallots and leek and gently fry for 5–8 minutes until softened. Add the potatoes and pour in the wine. Bubble for 2–3 minutes.

2 Stir in the chopped tomatoes, oregano, sugar, a little seasoning and 150ml (5fl oz) water. Simmer for 35 minutes, stirring occasionally, until the potatoes are tender.

3 Season the fish fillets and nestle them into the stew. Cover the pan and simmer gently for 5 minutes until the fish is cooked through. Stir gently to flake the fish, then check the seasoning. Sprinkle with basil and serve immediately.

Serves 4

Lentil Casserole

Hands-on time: 20 minutes
Cooking time: 1 hour

2 tbsp olive oil

2 onions, sliced

4 carrots, sliced

3 leeks, trimmed and sliced

450g (1lb) button mushrooms

2 garlic cloves, crushed

2.5cm (1in) piece fresh root ginger,
   peeled and grated

1 tbsp ground coriander

225g (8oz) split red lentils

750ml (1¼ pints) hot vegetable stock

4 tbsp freshly chopped coriander

salt and freshly ground black pepper

1 Preheat the oven to 180°C (160°C fan oven) mark 4. Heat the oil in a flameproof ovenproof casserole. Add the onions, carrots and leeks and fry, stirring, for 5 minutes. Add the mushrooms, garlic, ginger and ground coriander and fry for 2–3 minutes.

2 Rinse and drain the lentils, then stir into the casserole with the hot stock. Season with salt and ground black pepper and bring back to the boil. Cover and cook in the oven for 45–50 minutes until the vegetables and lentils are tender. Stir in the coriander before serving.

Serves 6

Classics

Chicken Tagine

Hands-on time: 15 minutes
Cooking time: about 25 minutes

1 tbsp vegetable oil
8 chicken drumsticks
½ tsp each ground cumin, coriander,
    cinnamon and paprika
75g (3oz) ready to eat dried apricots,
    finely chopped
40g (1½oz) raisins
400g can chopped tomatoes
75g (3oz) couscous
salt and freshly ground black pepper
a large handful of fresh coriander,
    chopped, to garnish

1 Heat the oil in a large flameproof casserole and brown the drumsticks well all over. Stir in the spices and cook for 1 minute. Add the apricots, raisins, tomatoes, 400ml (14fl oz) water and seasoning to taste, bring to the boil, reduce the heat and simmer for 10 minutes.

2 Stir in the couscous and simmer for 5 minutes more or until the couscous is tender and the chicken is cooked through. Check the seasoning. Sprinkle with chopped coriander and serve immediately.

Serves 4

Beef and Dumpling Stew

Hands-on time: 25 minutes
Cooking time: 3 hours 40 minutes

2 tbsp sunflower oil

450g (1lb) stewing steak, cut into 5cm (2in) pieces

2 medium onions, finely sliced

2 carrots, sliced

350g (12oz) swede, peeled and cut into chunks

2 tbsp plain flour

150ml (¼ pint) Irish dry stout

300ml (½ pint) hot beef stock

2 tsp dark brown sugar

1 tbsp Worcestershire sauce

1 bay leaf

1 fresh thyme sprig

For the dumplings

200g (7oz) plain flour

3 tsp baking powder

½ tsp dry English mustard

½ tsp salt

50g (2oz) low-fat vegetable suet

2 tbsp mixed freshly chopped herbs (we used parsley, sage, rosemary, and thyme)

1 Preheat the oven to 150°C (130°C fan oven) mark 2. Heat 1 tbsp oil in a flameproof casserole dish and brown the beef in batches. Put to one side.

2 Add the remaining oil to the pan and gently fry the onions and carrots for 10 minutes until softened. Add the swede and cook for 2 minutes.

3 Put the beef back into the pan, sprinkle in the flour and cook for 1 minute. Gradually stir in the Guinness and hot stock. Add the sugar, Worcestershire sauce, bay leaf and thyme, then bring to the boil. Cover and cook in the oven for 3 hours.

4 To make the dumplings, sift the flour, baking powder, mustard and salt into a bowl. Stir in the suet and mixed herbs. Using a flat-bladed knife, stir in about 150ml (¼ pint) cold water to make a soft but not too sticky dough.

Serves 6

5 Divide the dough into 12 and roll into balls. Drop on to the stew, spaced evenly apart. Cover and cook for 20 minutes until puffed up. Remove the lid and put back into the oven for 5 minutes to finish cooking the dumplings.

Liver Stroganoff

Hands-on time: 15 minutes
Cooking time: about 20 minutes

1 tsp vegetable or sunflower oil
2 shallots, finely chopped
250g (9oz) chestnut mushrooms, sliced
350g (12oz) calves' liver, cut into strips
25ml (1fl oz) brandy (optional)
1 tbsp wholegrain mustard
150g (5oz) half-fat crème fraîche
150g (5oz) 2% fat Greek yogurt
large handful baby spinach leaves
salt and freshly ground black pepper
crusty bread, mashed potatoes or boiled rice to serve

1 Heat the vegetable or sunflower oil in a large frying pan. Add the shallots and gently fry for 5 minutes. Turn up the heat to high and add the chestnut mushrooms. Fry for 5 minutes, or until the mushrooms have released their moisture, are tender and the pan is almost dry again.

2 Add the liver and fry, stirring occasionally, for 5 minutes. Carefully add the brandy, if you like, then stir in the mustard, crème fraîche and yogurt. Heat through (do not boil), then stir in the spinach and check the seasoning. Serve with crusty bread, mashed potatoes or boiled rice.

Serves 4

Classic Curry

Hands-on time: 5 minutes
Cooking time: about 25 minutes

1 tbsp vegetable oil
1 large onion, finely chopped
1 garlic clove, crushed
4cm (1½in) piece fresh root ginger,
   peeled and grated
1–2 green chillies, seeded and
   finely chopped
¼ tsp ground turmeric
1 tsp each ground coriander and
   ground cumin
160ml can coconut cream
100ml (3½fl oz) fish stock
500g (1lb 2oz) fresh tomatoes,
   roughly chopped
400g (14oz) raw king prawns, peeled
salt and freshly ground black pepper
2 tbsp freshly chopped coriander
   to garnish
boiled basmati rice or naan, lime
   wedges and chutney to serve

1 Heat the oil in a large pan, add the onion and gently fry for 10 minutes until softened. Add the garlic, ginger, chillies and spices and fry for 2 minutes.

2 Stir in the coconut cream and fish stock, followed by the chopped tomatoes. Season, bring to the boil, then leave to bubble for 5–10 minutes until the sauce has thickened.

3 Add the prawns, reduce the heat and simmer gently for 3 minutes until they turn pink – don't boil or they'll become tough. Check the seasoning and garnish with chopped coriander. Serve with boiled rice or naan, lime wedges and chutney.

Serves 4

Perfect Mussels

One of the most popular shellfish, mussels take moments to cook. Careful preparation is important, so give yourself enough time to get the shellfish ready.

Storing mussels

To store fresh mussels safely, keep in an open bag in the fridge, covered lightly with damp kitchen paper (do not submerge in water for prolonged periods of time). Before use, check to make sure the mussels are alive – the shells should be tightly closed (give them a sharp tap on a worksurface if they aren't, and discard any that haven't closed after 30 seconds or any that have broken shells).

Preparing mussels

1 Scrape off the fibres attached to the shells (beards). If the mussels are very clean, give them a quick rinse under the cold tap. If they are very sandy, scrub them with a stiff brush.

2 If the shells have sizeable barnacles on them, it is best (though not essential) to remove them. Rap them sharply with a metal spoon or the back of a washing-up brush, then scrape off.

1

Cooking mussels

1   Discard any open mussels that don't shut when sharply tapped; this means they are dead and could be dangerous to eat.

2   In a large heavy-based pan, fry 2 finely chopped shallots and a generous handful of parsley in 25g (1oz) butter for about 2 minutes or until soft. Pour in 1cm (½in) dry white wine.

3   Add the mussels to the pan and cover tightly with a lid. Steam for 5-10 minutes until the shells open. Immediately take the pan away from the heat.

4   Using a slotted spoon, remove the mussels from the pan and discard any that haven't opened, then boil the cooking liquid rapidly to reduce. Pour over the mussels and serve immediately.

2

3

Moules Marinière

Hands-on time: 15 minutes
Cooking time: 20 minutes

2kg (4½lb) fresh mussels, scrubbed, rinsed and beards removed (see page 70)

25g (1oz) butter

4 shallots, finely chopped

2 garlic cloves, crushed

200ml (7fl oz) dry white wine

2 tbsp freshly chopped flat-leafed parsley

100ml (3½fl oz) single cream

salt and freshly ground black pepper

crusty bread to serve

1 Tap the mussels on the worksurface, and discard any that do not close or that have broken shells. Heat the butter in a large non-stick lidded frying pan, and sauté the shallots over a medium-high heat for about 10 minutes until soft.

2 Add the garlic, wine and half the parsley to the pan, and bring to the boil. Tip in the mussels and reduce the heat a little. Cover and cook for about 5 minutes or until all the shells have opened; discard any mussels that don't open.

3 Lift out the mussels with a slotted spoon and put into serving bowls, and cover with foil to keep warm. Add the cream to the stock, season with salt and ground black pepper, and cook for 1–2 minutes to heat through. Pour a little sauce over the mussels and sprinkle with the rest of the parsley. Serve immediately with crusty bread.

Serves 4

Leek and Potato Soup

Hands-on time: 10 minutes
Cooking time: about 45 minutes

25g (1oz) butter
1 onion, finely chopped
1 garlic clove, crushed
550g (1¼lb) leeks, chopped
200g (7oz) floury potatoes,
  peeled and sliced
1.3 litres (2¼ pints) hot vegetable stock
crème fraîche and chopped chives
  to garnish

1 Melt the butter in a pan over a
  gentle heat. Add the onion and
  cook for 10–15 minutes until soft.
  Add the garlic and cook for a further
  1 minute. Add the leeks and cook
  for 5–10 minutes until softened.
  Add the potatoes and toss together
  with the leeks.
2 Pour in the hot stock and bring
  to the boil. Reduce the heat and
  simmer the soup for 20 minutes
  until the potatoes are tender.
  Leave to cool a little, then purée
  in a food processor.
3 Reheat before serving, garnished
  with crème fraîche and chives.

Serves 4

There are two main types of rice: long-grain and short-grain. Long-grain rice is generally served as an accompaniment, such as basmati rice in Indian cooking; the most commonly used type of long-grain rice in South-east Asian cooking is jasmine rice, also known as Thai fragrant rice. It has a distinctive taste and slightly sticky texture. There are various types of short-grain rice, including that used to make sushi. If you cook rice often, you may want to invest in a rice steamer. They are available from Asian supermarkets and some kitchen shops and give good, consistent results.

Thai rice

To serve six, you will need: 500g (1lb 2oz) Thai rice, a handful of fresh mint leaves, salt.

1 Cook the rice and mint in lightly salted boiling water for 10–12 minutes until tender. Drain well and serve.

Basmati rice

Put the rice into a bowl and cover with cold water. Stir until this becomes cloudy, then drain and repeat until the water is clear. Soak the rice for 30 minutes, then drain before cooking.

Long-grain rice

Long-grain rice needs no special preparation, although it should be washed to remove excess starch. Put the rice in a bowl and cover with cold water. Stir until this becomes cloudy, then drain and repeat until the water is clear. Use 50–75g (2–3oz) raw rice per person; measured by volume 50–75ml (2–2½fl oz).

1 Measure the rice by volume and put it into a pan with a pinch of salt and twice the volume of boiling water (or stock).

2 Bring to the boil. Reduce the heat to low and set the timer for the time stated on the pack. The rice should be al dente: tender with a bite at the centre.

3 When the rice is cooked, fluff up the grains with a fork.

Saffron rice

To serve eight, you will need:
500g (1lb 2oz) basmati rice,
900ml (1½ pints) stock made with
1½ chicken stock cubes, 5 tbsp
sunflower or light vegetable oil,
½ tsp saffron threads, salt, 75g (3oz)
blanched and coarsely chopped
almonds and pistachio nuts, to
garnish (optional).

1 Put the rice into a bowl and
   cover with warm water, then
   drain well through a sieve.
2 Put the stock, oil and a good
   pinch of salt into a pan, then
   cover and bring to the boil.
   Add the saffron and the rice.
3 Cover the pan and bring the
   stock back to the boil, then stir,
   reduce the heat to low, replace
   the lid and cook gently for
   10 minutes or until little holes
   appear all over the surface of the
   cooked rice and the grains are
   tender. Leave to stand, covered,
   for 15 minutes.
4 Fluff up the rice with a fork and
   transfer it to a warmed serving
   dish. Sprinkle the nuts on top of
   the rice, if you like, and serve.

Basic risotto

Italian risotto is made with
medium-grain Arborio, Vialone
Nano or Carnaroli rice, which
releases starch to give a rich,
creamy texture. It is traditionally
cooked on the hob, but can also
be cooked in the oven by adding
all the liquid in one go and cooking
until the liquid is absorbed.

To serve four, you will need:
1 chopped onion, 50g (2oz) butter,
900ml (1½ pints) chicken stock,
225g (8oz) risotto rice, 50g (2oz)
freshly grated Parmesan, plus
extra to serve.

1 Gently fry the onion in the butter
   for 10-15 minutes until very
   lightly coloured. Heat the stock
   in a separate pan and keep at
   a simmer. Add the rice to the
   butter and onion and stir for
   1-2 minutes until well coated.

1

2a

2 Add a ladleful of hot stock and stir constantly until absorbed. Add the remaining stock a ladleful at a time, stirring, until the rice is al dente (tender but still with bite at the centre). This will take 20–30 minutes – you may not need all the stock. Stir in the Parmesan and serve immediately with extra cheese.

2b

Beef Pilaf

Hands-on time: 10 minutes
Cooking time: about 40 minutes

1 tbsp vegetable oil
1 onion, finely sliced
450g (1lb) diced stewing beef
2 tbsp ground garam masala
200g (7oz) basmati rice
500ml (17fl oz) chicken stock
200g (7oz) fine green beans, trimmed
75g (3oz) dried apricots, chopped
4 tbsp mango chutney
salt and freshly ground black pepper

To garnish
25g (1oz) flaked almonds
freshly chopped parsley or coriander
   (optional)

1 Heat the oil in a large pan. Add the onion and fry for 8 minutes or until softened. Add the beef and fry for 10 minutes or until browned (add a splash of water if the pan looks too dry). Stir in the spice and rice and fry for 1 minute more.

2 Pour in the stock and bring to the boil, then reduce the heat right down, cover and simmer for 10 minutes.

3 Stir in the beans and apricots, then cover again and cook for 10 minutes more or until the stock is absorbed and the rice is tender. Fold in the chutney and season to taste with salt and ground black pepper. Garnish with flaked almonds and chopped parsley or coriander, if you like.

Serves 4

Paella

Hands-on time: 15 minutes
Cooking time: about 30 minutes

1 tbsp vegetable oil
1 large onion, thinly sliced
4 boneless, skinless chicken thighs,
  roughly chopped
2 garlic cloves, finely chopped
a pinch of saffron
¼ tsp smoked paprika
1 red pepper, seeded and finely diced
300g (11oz) paella rice
1.1 litres (2 pints) hot chicken stock
180g tub mussel meat, drained if
  in brine
a large handful of fresh curly parsley,
  roughly chopped
salt and freshly ground black pepper

1 Gently heat the oil in a large paella pan or frying pan. Add the onion and cook for 5 minutes. Add the chicken and cook for 3 minutes. Stir in the garlic, saffron and paprika and cook for 1 minute to release the flavours.

2 Stir in the red pepper and rice. Pour in the hot stock and leave to simmer gently for 20 minutes, stirring occasionally, or until the rice is cooked through.

3 Stir in the mussels and parsley and check the seasoning. Serve immediately.

Serves 4

Bacon and Squash Risotto

Hands-on time: 20 minutes
Cooking time: about 30 minutes

1 tbsp olive oil

200g (7oz) smoked bacon lardons

½ butternut squash, about 350g (12oz), peeled, halved, seeded and cut into 1.5cm (½in) cubes

1 onion, finely chopped

1 garlic clove, crushed

350g (12oz) risotto rice

150ml (5fl oz) white wine

1.1 litre (2 pints) hot vegetable stock

2 tbsp pesto

salt and freshly ground black pepper

1 Heat half the oil in a large pan over a medium heat. Fry the lardons for 5 minutes or until golden.

2 Use a slotted spoon to lift out the bacon and put into a large bowl. Add the remaining oil to the pan and fry the squash and onion for 10 minutes until tender. Stir in the garlic and cook for 1 minute. Lift the squash mixture out of the pan and add to the bacon.

3 Put the empty pan back on to the heat and add the rice and wine. Bring to the boil, reduce the heat and simmer, stirring, for 2 minutes. Gradually add the hot stock a ladleful at a time, adding each ladleful only when the previous one has been absorbed. Stir well after each addition. Continue until the rice is cooked – about 15 minutes.

4 Stir the bacon mixture into the risotto and swirl through the pesto. Check the seasoning, then serve immediately.

Saffron and Red Pepper Risotto

Hands-on time: 20 minutes
Cooking time: about 20 minutes

1 tbsp extra virgin olive oil, plus extra
  to drizzle

300g (11oz) risotto rice

2 large pinches of saffron

150ml (5fl oz) white wine

200g (7oz) roughly chopped roasted
  red peppers

50g (2oz) rocket

salt and freshly ground black pepper

1 Heat the oil in a large pan over a medium heat. Add the risotto rice and saffron and fry for 1 minute, then add the white wine and leave to bubble until most of the liquid has been absorbed.

2 Measure 800ml (1¼ pint) boiling water into a large heatproof jug. Add a ladleful of this water to the rice pan and stir until the water has been fully absorbed. Continue this process until the rice is cooked, about 15–18 minutes.

3 Stir through the roasted red peppers and check the seasoning. Serve immediately, topped with rocket and a drizzle of extra virgin olive oil.

Serves 4

Veggie Pots

Keep It Seasonal

Why? Because not only will the produce you buy taste fantastic, it will also cost less. Look out for good deals at supermarkets, farm shops, markets and greengrocers where you can sometimes buy larger, cheaper quantities for freezing or batch cooking. Pick Your Own farms often charge half the price of the supermarkets. You can pick fruit and vegetables at their ripest and enjoy a fun day out with the family too.

Month	Vegetables	Fruit
JANUARY	Beetroot, Brussels sprouts, cauliflower, celeriac, celery, chicory, Jerusalem artichoke, kale, leeks, parsnips, potatoes (maincrop), rhubarb, swede, turnips	Apples, clementines, kiwi fruit, lemons, oranges, passion fruit, pears, pineapples, pomegranates, satsumas, tangerines, walnuts
FEBRUARY	Brussels sprouts, cauliflower, celeriac, chicory, kale, leeks, parsnips, potatoes (maincrop), rhubarb, swede	Bananas, blood oranges, kiwi fruit, lemons, oranges, passion fruit, pears, pineapples, pomegranates
MARCH	Cauliflower, chicory, kale, leeks, purple sprouting broccoli, rhubarb, spring onions	Bananas, blood oranges, kiwi fruit, lemons, oranges, passion fruit, pineapples, pomegranates
APRIL	Asparagus, broccoli, Jersey royal potatoes, purple sprouting broccoli, radishes, rhubarb, rocket, spinach, spring onions, watercress	Bananas, kiwi fruit
MAY	Asparagus, broccoli, Jersey royal potatoes, new potatoes, radishes, rhubarb, rocket, spinach, spring onions, watercress	Cherries, kiwi fruit, strawberries
JUNE	Artichokes, asparagus, aubergines, broad beans, broccoli, carrots, courgettes, fennel, mangetouts, Jersey royal potatoes, new potatoes, peas, radishes, rocket, runner beans, spring onions, turnips, watercress	Cherries, strawberries

Month	Vegetables	Fruit
JULY	Artichokes, aubergines, beetroot, broad beans, broccoli, carrots, courgettes, cucumber, fennel, French beans, garlic, mangetouts, new potatoes, onions, peas, potatoes (maincrop), radishes, rocket, runner beans, turnips, watercress	Apricots, blackberries, blueberries, cherries, gooseberries, greengages, kiwi fruit, melons, peaches, raspberries, redcurrants, strawberries, tomatoes
AUGUST	Artichokes, aubergines, beetroot, broad beans, broccoli, carrots, courgettes, cucumber, fennel, French beans, garlic, leeks, mangetouts, marrow, new potatoes, onions, peas, peppers, potatoes (maincrop), radishes, rocket, runner beans, sweetcorn, watercress	Apricots, blackberries, blueberries, damsons, greengages, kiwi fruit, melons, nectarines, peaches, plums, raspberries, redcurrants, tomatoes
SEPTEMBER	Artichokes, aubergines, beetroot, broccoli, butternut squash, carrots, courgettes, cucumber, fennel, garlic, leeks, mangetout, marrow, onions, parsnips, peas, peppers, potatoes (maincrop), radishes, rocket, runner beans, sweetcorn, watercress, wild mushrooms	Apples, blackberries, damsons, figs, grapes, melons, nectarines, peaches, pears, plums, raspberries, redcurrants, tomatoes, walnuts
OCTOBER	Artichokes, beetroot, broccoli, butternut squash, carrots, celeriac, celery, fennel, kale, leeks, marrow, onions, parsnips, potatoes (maincrop), pumpkin, swede, turnips, watercress, wild mushrooms	Apples, chestnuts, figs, pears, quince, tomatoes, walnuts
NOVEMBER	Artichokes, beetroot, Brussels sprouts, celeriac, celery, chicory, kale, leeks, parsnips, potatoes (maincrop), pumpkin, swede, turnips, watercress, wild mushrooms	Apples, chestnuts, clementines, cranberries, figs, passion fruit, pears, quince, satsumas, tangerines, walnuts
DECEMBER	Beetroot, Brussels sprouts, cauliflower, celeriac, celery, chicory, kale, leeks, parsnips, potatoes (maincrop), pumpkin, swede, turnips	Apples, chestnuts, clementines, cranberries, passion fruit, pears, pineapple, pomegranate, satsumas, tangerines, walnuts

Summer Vegetable Soup
with Herb Pistou

Hands-on time: 20 minutes
Cooking time: 1 hour

3 tbsp sunflower oil

1 onion, finely chopped

225g (8oz) waxy potatoes, finely diced

175g (6oz) carrots, finely diced

1 medium turnip, finely diced

4 bay leaves

6 large fresh sage leaves

2 courgettes, about 375g (13oz), finely diced

175g (6oz) green beans, trimmed and halved

125g (4oz) shelled small peas

225g (8oz) tomatoes, seeded and finely diced

1 small broccoli head, broken into florets

salt and freshly ground black pepper

pistou or ready-made pesto to serve

1 Heat the oil in a large pan over a gentle heat. Add the onion, potatoes, carrots and turnip, and cook for 10 minutes. Pour in 1.7 litres (3 pints) cold water, season with salt and ground black pepper, bring to the boil and add the bay and sage leaves. Reduce the heat and simmer for 25 minutes.

2 Add the courgettes, beans, peas and tomatoes. Bring back to the boil, reduce the heat and simmer for 10–15 minutes. Add the broccoli 5 minutes before the end of the cooking time.

3 Remove the bay and sage leaves and adjust the seasoning. Pour the soup into warmed bowls and serve immediately; serve the pistou or pesto separately to stir into the hot soup.

Serves 6

Broad Bean and Feta Salad

Hands-on time: 10 minutes
Cooking time: 5 minutes

225g (8oz) podded broad beans
100g (3½oz) feta, chopped
2 tbsp freshly chopped mint
2 tbsp extra virgin olive oil
a squeeze of lemon juice
salt and freshly ground black pepper
lemon wedges to serve (optional)

1 Cook the beans in salted boiling water for 3–5 minutes until tender. Drain, then plunge them into cold water and drain again. Remove their skins, if you like.

2 Tip the beans into a bowl, add the feta, mint, oil and a squeeze of lemon juice. Season well with salt and ground black pepper and toss together. Serve with lemon wedges, if you like.

Serves 2

Warm Spiced Rice Salad

Hands-on time: 10 minutes
Cooking time: about 30 minutes

½ tbsp ground cumin
½ tsp ground cinnamon
2 tbsp sunflower oil
2 large red onions, sliced
250g (9oz) basmati rice
600ml (1 pint) hot vegetable or
   chicken stock
400g can lentils, drained and rinsed
salt and freshly ground black pepper

For the salad

75g (3oz) watercress
250g (9oz) broccoli, steamed and
   chopped into 2.5cm (1in) pieces
25g (1oz) sultanas
75g (3oz) dried apricots, chopped
75g (3oz) mixed nuts and seeds
2 tbsp freshly chopped flat-leafed
   parsley
100g (3½oz) goat's cheese, crumbled

1 Put the cumin and cinnamon into a large deep frying pan and heat gently for 1–2 minutes. Add the oil and onions and fry over a low heat for 8–10 minutes until the onions are soft. Add the rice, toss to coat in the spices and onions, then add the hot stock. Cover and cook for 12–15 minutes until the stock has been absorbed and the rice is cooked. Season, tip into a serving bowl and add the lentils.

2 To make the salad, add the watercress, broccoli, sultanas, apricots and mixed nuts and seeds to the bowl. Scatter with the parsley, then toss together, top with the cheese and serve immediately.

Serves 4

Easy Veggie Pad Thai

Hands-on time: 15 minutes
Cooking time: 10 minutes

2 tbsp groundnut oil

2 medium eggs, beaten

2 spring onions, cut into chunks

¼ red chilli, chopped

1 red pepper, seeded and finely sliced

1 carrot, finely sliced

1 garlic clove, crushed

juice of ½ lime

1 tbsp tamarind paste

125g (4oz) bean sprouts

200g (7oz) straight-to-wok
  ribbon noodles

a handful each of freshly chopped
  coriander and mint

2 tbsp roasted peanuts, chopped

salt and freshly ground black pepper

1 Heat 1 tbsp oil in a wok or non-stick
  pan. Add the eggs, then stir-fry until
  just set. Season with salt and ground
  black pepper, then scoop out and
  put to one side.

2 Heat the remaining 1 tbsp oil in
  the wok and add the spring onions,
  chilli, red pepper, carrot and garlic.
  Stir-fry for 3–5 minutes, adding a
  splash of water if you need to.

3 Stir in the lime juice and tamarind,
  then add the bean sprouts, cooked
  egg and noodles. Mix well and
  heat through. Sprinkle with the
  herbs and peanuts and serve.

Serves 2

Egg and Pepper Pizza

Hands-time: 15 minutes
Cooking time: 12 minutes

150g (5oz) red and yellow marinated peppers in oil

8 tbsp passata

4 small pizza bases

4 medium eggs

125g (4oz) watercress, washed and stalks removed

1 Preheat the oven to 220°C (200°C fan oven) mark 7 and preheat two large baking sheets, big enough to hold two pizzas each.

2 Drain the peppers, keeping the oil to one side. Chop into thin strips. Spoon 2 tbsp passata over each pizza base and scatter strips of the chopped peppers around the edges.

3 Make a dip in the passata in the middle of each pizza and break an egg into it. Carefully slide the pizzas on to the preheated baking sheets and cook in the oven for 12 minutes until the egg is thoroughly cooked.

4 Top the pizzas with the watercress, drizzle with a little of the reserved oil from the peppers and serve.

Serves 4

Vegetable Frittata

🍴 **Hands-on time:** 15 minutes
Cooking time: 25 minutes

15g (½oz) butter
1 red onion, finely sliced
2 green peppers, seeded and finely sliced
200g (7oz) cherry tomatoes
8 medium eggs
2 tbsp fresh chopped mint
25g (1oz) mature Cheddar, grated
salt and freshly ground black pepper
green salad to serve

1 Melt the butter in a 23cm (9in) frying pan. Add the onion and peppers and gently fry for 10 minutes, adding a splash of water if the pan looks a little dry. Add the cherry tomatoes and fry for 2–3 minutes.

2 Preheat the grill to medium. In a large bowl, beat together the eggs and most of the mint. Season well with salt and ground black pepper. Pour the egg mixture into the frying pan and use a wooden spoon to spread the mixture evenly between the vegetables. Cook on the hob over a low heat for 5 minutes until the egg is set around the edges.

3 Sprinkle over the grated cheese. Grill for 5 minutes or until the egg is cooked and the cheese is golden and bubbling. Sprinkle with the remaining mint, cut the frittata into wedges and serve hot or at room temperature with a green salad.

Serves 4

Black-eye Bean Chilli

Hands-on time: 10 minutes
Cooking time: 20 minutes

1 tbsp olive oil
1 onion, chopped
3 celery sticks, finely chopped
2 × 400g cans black-eye beans, drained
2 × 400g cans chopped tomatoes
2 or 3 splashes of Tabasco sauce
3 tbsp freshly chopped coriander
warm tortillas and soured cream
  to serve

1 Heat the oil in a heavy-based frying pan over a low heat. Add the onion and celery and fry for 10 minutes or until softened.
2 Add the black-eye beans to the pan with the tomatoes and Tabasco sauce. Bring to the boil, then reduce the heat and simmer for 10 minutes.
3 Just before serving, stir in the chopped coriander. Spoon the chilli on to warm tortillas and serve with a spoonful of soured cream.

Serves 4

Mauritian Vegetable Curry

Hands-on time: 15 minutes
Cooking time: 30 minutes

3 tbsp vegetable oil

1 onion, finely sliced

4 garlic cloves, crushed

2.5cm (1in) piece fresh root ginger, peeled and grated

3 tbsp medium curry powder

6 fresh curry leaves

150g (5oz) potatoes, cut into 1cm (½in) cubes

125g (4oz) aubergine, cut into 2cm (¾in) sticks, 5mm (¼in) wide

150g (5oz) carrots, cut into 5mm (¼in) dice

900ml (1½ pints) hot vegetable stock

a pinch of saffron

1 tsp salt

150g (5oz) green beans, trimmed

75g (3oz) frozen peas

freshly ground black pepper

3 tbsp freshly chopped coriander to garnish

1 Heat the oil in a large heavy-based pan over a low heat. Add the onion and fry for 5–10 minutes until golden. Add the garlic, ginger, curry powder and curry leaves and fry for a further minute.

2 Add the potatoes and aubergine to the pan and fry, stirring, for 2 minutes. Add the carrots, hot stock, saffron and salt. Season with ground black pepper. Cover and cook for 10 minutes or until the vegetables are almost tender.

3 Add the beans and peas to the pan and cook for a further 4 minutes. Sprinkle with the chopped coriander and serve.

Serves 4

Perfect Veg

Nutritious, mouth-watering and essential to a healthy diet –
vegetables are ideal for adding to slow-cooked dishes.

Stewing

1. Cut the vegetables into large bite-size pieces, no more than about 5cm (2in) square. Put them into a heatproof casserole (for oven cooking) or a heavy-based pan (for hob cooking). Add salt and ground black pepper and flavourings, if you like (see Perfect stews opposite), and mix well.

2. Preheat the oven to 180°C (160°C fan oven) mark 4 if you are cooking in the oven.

3. Pour in enough hot stock to come about three-quarters of the way up the vegetables. Cover the dish with a lid or foil and cook for 30–40 minutes until the vegetables are tender but not disintegrating. Turn the vegetables once during cooking and baste with the juices a few times.

Perfect stews

- ☐ Any vegetable can be stewed; be careful not to overcook it
- ☐ Ideal flavourings for stewed vegetables include garlic, shallots, curry powder (or Indian spices), and chilli sauce or chopped chilli
- ☐ Potatoes will thicken the dish a little as they release some of their starch

Braising

1. Prepare the vegetables (see Perfect braising). Pack tightly in a single layer in an ovenproof dish. Preheat the oven to 180°C (160°C fan oven) mark 4. Dot the vegetables generously with butter and season with salt.
2. Pour in enough hot stock to come halfway up the vegetables. Cover the dish with a lid or foil and cook for 30-40 minutes until the vegetables are soft. Baste them with the buttery stock a few times during cooking.

Perfect braising

- ☐ Carrots, fennel, leeks, celeriac, celery and cabbage are all good braised
- ☐ Leave vegetables whole or cut them into chunks. Shred cabbage, then fry lightly before braising
- ☐ Cook all the vegetables in a single layer

2

Rich Aubergine Stew

Hands-on time: 25 minutes
Cooking time: about 30 minutes

1 tbsp extra virgin olive oil, plus extra
  to drizzle

3 medium aubergines, cut into
  2.5cm (1in) pieces

1 onion, roughly chopped

2 celery sticks, roughly chopped

1 red pepper, seeded and roughly
  chopped

400g can chopped tomatoes

100g (3½oz) green olives, pitted

1 tsp caster sugar

1 tbsp red wine vinegar

a large handful of fresh parsley,
  chopped

50g (2oz) raisins (optional)

salt and freshly ground black pepper

crusty bread to serve

1 Heat the oil in a large pan and cook
  the aubergines for 10–12 minutes
  until brown and almost tender. Add
  the onion, celery, red pepper and a
  splash of water and fry for 5 minutes.

2 Add the tomatoes, olives and
  some seasoning and simmer for
  10 minutes or until the aubergine
  is completely tender.

3 Stir in the sugar, vinegar, parsley
  and the raisins, if you like. Drizzle
  with extra oil, if you like, and serve
  warm or at room temperature with
  some crusty bread.

Roasted Vegetable, Lentil and Halloumi Bake

Hands-on time: 20 minutes
Cooking time: 45 minutes

2 red peppers, seeded and
   roughly chopped
200g (7oz) closed cup mushrooms,
   thickly sliced
2 large sweet potatoes, cut into
   2.5cm (1in) chunks
1 courgette, thickly sliced
2 tbsp olive oil
150g (5oz) red lentils, rinsed
1 litre (1¾ pint) hot vegetable stock
250g pack vegetarian halloumi,
   thickly sliced
a large handful of fresh curly parsley,
   finely chopped
crusty bread to serve

1 Preheat the oven to 200°C (180°C fan oven) mark 6. Put the vegetables into a large roasting tin, drizzle over the oil and season well with salt and ground black pepper. Mix everything together.

2 Roast the vegetables for 25 minutes until they are almost tender. Sprinkle over the lentils, then pour over the hot stock. Continue to roast for a further 15 minutes until the lentils and vegetables are cooked through.

3 Preheat the grill to high. Lay the halloumi slices on top of the roasted vegetables and grill for 2–3 minutes until golden. Sprinkle over the finely chopped parsley and serve in gently warmed bowls with crusty bread.

Serves 4

The Vegetarian Family

Whether your family are already committed vegetarians or are thinking of giving up meat and fish altogether, it is essential that everyone gets a good balanced diet.

Vegetarian children

From the age of one, your child should be eating (or at least be offered) three small meals a day, along with a mid-morning and a mid-afternoon snack (which could be a glass of milk, some chopped fruit or a piece of cheese). From the age of two, your child can eat much the same as the rest of the family. Avoid nuts unless they are ground into nut butter because there is danger of choking. The Department of Health advises that children should not be given soft-cooked eggs. So make sure that poached eggs are cooked until the yolk is set, and avoid giving children soft scrambled eggs and runny omelettes.

Feeding vegetarian teenagers

Adolescents need a nutrient-rich diet with lots of calories (girls about 2,100, boys about 2,800 per day). A varied vegetarian diet will easily provide this. Teenage girls should ensure they eat plenty of iron-rich foods. Encourage them to eat vitamin C and iron-rich foods together. Vegan adolescents should eat cereals and yeast extracts fortified with vitamin B12.

For some families, a non-meat-eater in their midst can cause problems at meal times. It's important to view this as a positive move for the family as a whole rather than as a problem. There's no doubt that the consumption of too much animal idea to use the opportunity to introduce more meat-free meals to all members of the household.

Making meals based on rice, potatoes and pasta is a good way to start. It's easy to cook simple nutritious vegetarian meals using these as a base combined with beans, lentils and well-flavoured ingredients such as garlic, tomato, spices, herbs and fresh vegetables.

Tasty risottos, pilafs, vegetable gratins and stuffed baked potatoes are delicious and would usually be made without meat anyway. For particularly steadfast carnivorous members of the family, serve these with grilled meat or fish or sliced cold meat as a last resort until the appeal of vegetarianism sinks in.

Pizzas are surprisingly quick and easy to make and are loved by most teenagers. Piled high with vegetables and served with a large mixed salad, they make a splendid supper. A chunky soup made from a mixture of vegetables and beans or lentils, served with hot garlic bread and followed by yogurt and fruit also makes a healthy meal.

Meat substitutes such as Quorn, and soya products like soya mince are useful additions to the new vegetarian cook's repertoire. Use them to make meat-free versions of traditional family favourites such as shepherd's pie, lasagne, spaghetti bolognese, kebabs and curry.

Suppers
to Share

Planning Ahead

Clever use of the fridge, freezer and storecupboard makes life easier and shopping trips fewer.

Change your shopping habits

❑ Do a big supermarket shop once a month for non-perishables – even better, order your shopping on-line to avoid impulse buys and keep an eye on the running total before you place the order. Some delivery companies offer free delivery at less popular times

❑ Only buy special offers or BOGOFs (buy one, get one free) if you have time to batch cook or space to freeze the extra

❑ Avoid ready-meals and ready-prepared ingredients, such as chopped onions – you are paying more for convenience

Before you go shopping

❑ Can you delay your food shop for another day? Check the storecupboard, fridge or freezer for ingredients that can make another meal

❑ Check the diary and plan the week's menu according to family activities

❑ Do a quick weekly stock-take of the storecupboard, fridge and freezer. Can ingredients near their use-by or best-before date be incorporated into the week's menu?

❑ Don't forget nature's free storecupboard – blackberries in hedgerows, sweet chestnuts and sloes, for example

The weekly menu

This needn't be a hefty document, simply jot down:

- ❑ An idea for every day of the week, including some dishes that you've already made and stored in the fridge or freezer
- ❑ Some recipes that make creative use of leftovers
- ❑ Some recipes that stretch – spaghetti bolognese tonight, chilli tomorrow
- ❑ Some quick meals that need a trip to the shops for one or two fresh ingredients
- ❑ Include vegetables or other accompaniments in your plan, but remember that you can always change your mind if you find a good bargain in the supermarket
- ❑ Rethink your approach to cooking – meat and fish are expensive, so you could make one or two nights a week

When you're shopping

- ❑ Tuck a notebook in your bag listing ingredients for family favourites and you'll be ready to take advantage of special offers on expensive ingredients such as meat and poultry
- ❑ Make a shopping list and stick to it
- ❑ Keep it seasonal
- ❑ Does the product cost less whole or in portions – for example, it's cheaper to:
  - buy a whole chicken and joint it into pieces yourself.
  - cut a whole salmon into fillets or steaks, then freeze in portions
- ❑ Compare the price per kilo. Loose fruit and vegetables can cost considerably less than pre-packed versions, for example

Roast Chicken with Apricot and Orange

Hands-on time: 15 minutes
Cooking time: 40 minutes

3 large carrots, cut into rough
 2cm (¾in) pieces
2 red onions, each cut into 8 wedges
½ tbsp cumin seeds
1 tbsp olive oil
zest and juice of 1 orange
8 boneless skinless chicken
 thigh fillets
50g (2oz) ready to eat dried apricots,
 chopped
salt and freshly ground black pepper
couscous, salad or crusty bread
 to serve

1 Preheat the oven to 200°C (180°C fan oven) mark 6. Put the carrots, onions, cumin, oil, orange zest and juice, a splash of water and seasoning into a roasting tin and toss together.

2 Roast for 15 minutes until the carrots are beginning to soften. Add the chicken and dried apricots and cook for a further 25 minutes until the chicken is cooked through and the vegetables are tender. Serve with couscous, salad or some crusty bread to mop up the juices.

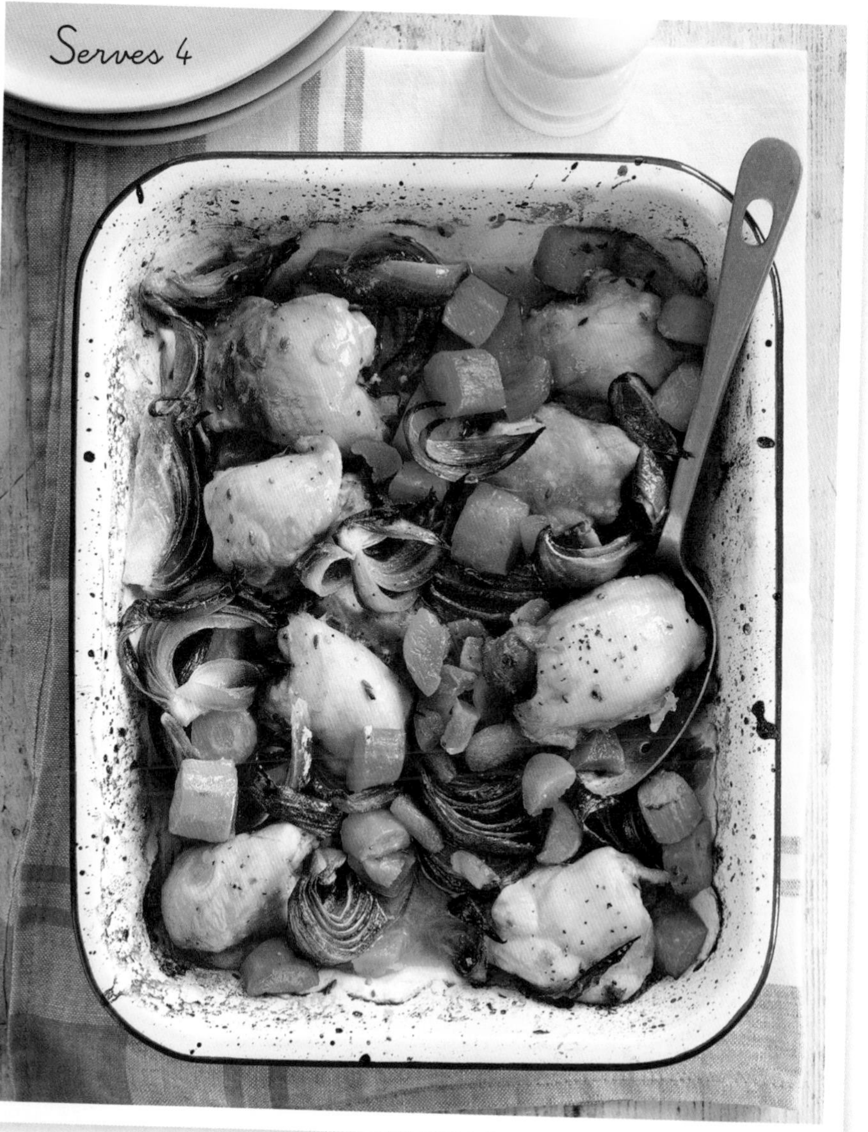
Serves 4

Chicken Tarragon

Hands-on time: 15 minutes
Cooking time: about 15 minutes

4 × 125g (4oz) chicken breasts,
   cut into bite-size pieces
25g (1oz) plain flour
2 tbsp olive oil
250g (9oz) chestnut mushrooms,
   sliced
150ml (5fl oz) white wine
300ml (½ pint) crème fraîche
½ tbsp Dijon mustard
2 tbsp freshly chopped tarragon
a large handful of spinach
salt and freshly ground black pepper
crusty bread to serve

1 Put the chicken into a bowl and sprinkle over the flour and some seasoning. Mix together. Heat half of the oil in a large frying pan over a medium-high heat. Brown the chicken for 5 minutes until golden – do this in batches if necessary to stop the chicken from sweating. Remove from the pan and put to one side.

2 Add the remaining oil to the pan and fry the mushrooms for 3–5 minutes until nearly cooked through. Put the chicken and any juices back into the pan. Pour over the wine and simmer for 2 minutes, then stir in the crème fraîche, mustard and most of the tarragon. Bring to the boil, reduce the heat and simmer for 5 minutes or until the chicken is cooked through.

3 Stir in the spinach and check the seasoning. Sprinkle over the remaining tarragon and serve with crusty bread to mop up the juices.

Serves 4

Mediterranean Sausage Roast

Hands-on time: 15 minutes
Cooking time: 40 minutes

8 pork sausages

1 red onion, cut into 8 wedges

1 tbsp roughly chopped oregano (or
use ½ tbsp dried oregano), plus
extra to garnish

5 garlic cloves, skin on

3 medium sweet potatoes, about 500g
(1lb 2oz), cut into 2.5cm (1in) chunks

2 tbsp extra virgin olive oil

3 tomatoes, cut into wedges

50g (2oz) black olives, pitted

salt and freshly ground black pepper

crusty bread to serve (optional)

1 Preheat the oven to 200°C (180°C
fan oven) mark 6. Put the sausages
into a large roasting tin and add
the onion wedges, oregano, garlic,
sweet potatoes, oil and plenty
of seasoning. Toss everything
together, then roast for 30 minutes.

2 Add the tomato wedges and black
olives and put back into the oven
for 10 minutes. Garnish with extra
oregano and, if you like, serve with
some crusty bread.

Serves 4

Easy Peasy Pork Chops

Hands-on time: 10 minutes
Cooking time: 40 minutes

4 pork loin chops
½ tbsp sunflower oil
400g (14oz) new potatoes, halved
  lengthways
2 apples, cored and cut into 8 wedges
75ml (3fl oz) each cider and hot
  vegetable stock
50g (2oz) blue Wensleydale cheese
salt and freshly ground black pepper
1 tbsp roughly chopped sage leaves,
  to garnish

1 Preheat the oven to 230°C (210°C fan oven) mark 8. Snip the fat on the pork chops at 2cm (¾in) intervals with a pair of scissors – this will stop the chops curling as they cook. Heat the oil in a flameproof roasting tin set over a medium heat on the hob, then brown the chops on both sides and put to one side.

2 Put the potatoes in the same roasting tin and coat in the oil. Roast for 15 minutes.

3 Nestle the chops and apples among the potatoes, then pour in the cider and hot stock. Season. Put back into the oven for 15 minutes or until the pork is cooked through.

4 Crumble over the cheese and put back into the oven for 2–3 minutes until melted. Garnish with sage and spoon over the cooking juices to serve.

Lamb and Pasta Pot

Hands-on time: 10 minutes
Cooking time: 50 minutes

1 half leg of lamb roasting joint – about
   1.1kg (2½lb) total weight
125g (4oz) smoked streaky bacon,
   chopped
150ml (¼ pint) red wine
400g can chopped tomatoes with
   chilli, or 400g (14oz) passata
75g (3oz) pasta shapes
12 sunblush tomatoes
150g (5oz) chargrilled artichokes
   in oil, drained and halved
a handful of fresh basil to garnish

1 Preheat the oven to 200°C (180°C
  fan oven) mark 6. Put the lamb and
  bacon into a small deep roasting
  tin and fry for 5 minutes or until
  the lamb is brown all over and the
  bacon is beginning to crisp.

2 Remove the lamb and put to one
  side. Pour the wine into the tin
  with the bacon – it should bubble
  immediately. Stir well, scraping
  the bottom of the tin to loosen any
  crusty bits, then leave to bubble
  until half the wine has evaporated.
  Stir in 300ml (½ pint) water and add
  the chopped tomatoes or passata,
  the pasta and sunblush tomatoes.

3 Put the lamb on a rack over the
  roasting tin so that the juices drip
  into the pasta. Cook, uncovered, in
  the oven for about 35 minutes.

4 Stir the artichokes into the pasta and
  put everything back in the oven for
  5 minutes or until the lamb is tender
  and the pasta cooked. Slice the lamb
  thickly and serve with the pasta,
  garnished with basil leaves.

Beef Quesadillas

Hands-on time: 20 minutes
Cooking time: about 45 minutes

½ tbsp vegetable oil
5 spring onions, finely sliced
400g (14oz) lean beef mince
few dashes Tabasco sauce
¼ tsp paprika
1 garlic clove, finely sliced
2 × 400g cans chopped tomatoes
8 flour tortillas
125g (4oz) mature Cheddar, grated
a large handful of fresh coriander,
   roughly chopped
salt and freshly ground black pepper
lime wedges and soured cream
   to serve

1 Heat the oil in a large frying pan. Add the spring onions and fry for 3–5 minutes until just softened. Empty into a large bowl. Brown the beef over a high heat for 5 minutes until cooked through. Stir in the Tabasco, paprika and garlic and cook for 1 minute. Add the tomatoes and some seasoning and simmer for 10 minutes. Tip the beef mixture into the bowl with the spring onions.

2 Wipe the pan clean, then put back on to a medium heat. Put a tortilla in the pan, then spoon over a quarter each of the beef mixture, cheese and coriander. Top with another tortilla and heat through for 3 minutes.

3 Using a spatula, flip the quesadilla and cook on the other side for 3 minutes. Slide on to a board, then cover with foil. Repeat with the remaining tortillas. Serve quartered, with lime wedges and soured cream.

Serves 4

Spicy Beef

Hands-on time: 10 minutes
Cooking time: 40 minutes

2 tsp sunflower oil

1 large onion, roughly chopped

1 garlic clove, finely chopped

1 small fresh red chilli, finely chopped

2 red peppers, roughly chopped

2 celery sticks, diced

400g (14oz) lean beef mince

400g can chopped tomatoes

2 × 400g cans mixed beans, drained
  and rinsed

1–2 tsp Tabasco sauce

2–3 tbsp roughly chopped fresh
  coriander to garnish (optional)

salsa and soft flour tortillas or basmati
  rice to serve

1 Heat the oil in a large heavy-based frying pan over a medium heat. Add the onion with 2 tbsp water and cook for 10 minutes or until soft. Add the garlic and chilli, and cook for a further 1–2 minutes until golden. Add the red peppers and celery, and cook for 5 minutes.

2 Add the beef to the pan and brown all over. Add the tomatoes, beans and Tabasco sauce, then simmer for 20 minutes. Garnish with coriander, if you like, and serve with salsa and tortillas or rice.

Serves 4

Salmon and Bulgur Wheat Pilau

Hands-on time: 5 minutes
Cooking time: 20 minutes

1 tbsp olive oil

1 onion, chopped

175g (6oz) bulgur wheat

450ml (¾ pint) vegetable stock

400g can pink salmon, drained
and flaked

125g (4oz) spinach, roughly chopped

225g (8oz) frozen peas

zest and juice of 1 lemon

salt and freshly ground black pepper

1 Heat the oil in a large pan. Add the onion and cook until softened. Stir in the bulgur wheat to coat in the oil, then stir in the stock and bring to the boil. Cover the pan, reduce the heat and simmer for 10–15 minutes until the stock has been fully absorbed.

2 Stir in the salmon, spinach, peas and lemon juice and cook until the spinach has wilted and the salmon and peas are heated through. Season with salt and ground black pepper and sprinkle with lemon zest before serving.

Prawn Gumbo

Hands-on time: 20 minutes
Cooking time: about 45 minutes

1 tbsp vegetable oil

1 medium onion, finely sliced

2 celery sticks, finely chopped

2 green peppers, seeded and roughly
  chopped

1–2 red chillies, to taste, seeded
  and finely chopped

3 thyme sprigs

2 garlic cloves, crushed

2 × 400g cans chopped tomatoes

200g (7oz) okra, roughly chopped

1 litre (1¾ pint) vegetable stock

150g (5oz) basmati rice, rinsed

300g (11oz) cooked, peeled king
  prawns

salt and freshly ground black pepper

a large handful of fresh flat-leafed
  parsley, roughly chopped, to garnish

1 Heat the oil in a large pan. Add
   the onion, celery and peppers
   and gently fry for 5 minutes until
   beginning to soften. Stir in the
   chillies, thyme, garlic, tomatoes,
   okra and stock. Bring to the boil,
   then reduce the heat and simmer
   for 20 minutes.

2 Stir in the rice, reduce the heat and
   simmer for 20 minutes, stirring
   occasionally, until the rice is cooked
   and the liquid has been absorbed.
   Stir in the prawns, heat through
   and check the seasoning. Discard
   the thyme sprigs, garnish with the
   parsley and serve.

Serves 4

Goat's Cheese and Onion Slice

Hands-on time: 10 minutes
Cooking time: 30 minutes

375g pack ready-rolled puff pastry
4 tbsp caramelised red onion relish
  or red onion marmalade
125g (4oz) marinated artichoke pieces
125g (4oz) cherry tomatoes, halved
100g (3½oz) button mushrooms,
  halved
50g (2oz) goat's cheese
1 tbsp extra virgin olive oil
salt and freshly ground black pepper
a large handful of rocket to garnish

1 Preheat the oven to 200°C (180°C fan oven) mark 6. Unroll the pastry and lay on a baking tray. Use a knife to score a border 2cm (¾in) from the edges – but don't cut through. Prick the inside border with a fork and cook for 8–10 minutes until the pastry starts to puff.

2 Take out of the oven and press down the pastry inside the border. Spread the relish or marmalade inside the border. Scatter over the artichokes, tomatoes and mushrooms. Crumble over the goat's cheese and drizzle over the oil. Season with salt and ground black pepper.

3 Put back into the oven for 15–20 minutes until the pastry has risen and is golden. Garnish with rocket and serve.

Serves 4

Sparkling Risotto

Hands-on time: 20 minutes
Cooking time: about 35 minutes

25g (1oz) butter

2 shallots, finely chopped

300g (11oz) risotto rice

350ml (12fl oz) sparkling wine

800ml (1⅓ pint) hot vegetable stock

100g (3½oz) mascarpone cheese

25g (1oz) Parmesan, finely grated
    (vegetarian, if needed)

salt and freshly ground black pepper

freshly grated nutmeg and gold leaf
    (optional) to garnish

1 Melt the butter in a large pan.
   Add the shallots and gently fry for
   10 minutes until softened. Stir in
   the rice and cook for 2 minutes until
   the rice turns translucent. Add the
   sparkling wine, then bring to the
   boil, reduce the heat and simmer,
   stirring, for 30 seconds.

2 Gradually add the hot stock a
   ladleful at a time, adding each
   ladleful only when the previous one
   has been absorbed. Stir well after
   each addition. Continue until the
   rice is nearly cooked – this will take
   about 20 minutes.

3 Once the rice is cooked through,
   stir in the mascarpone cheese and
   Parmesan. Check the seasoning,
   then spoon into warmed bowls and
   garnish with grated nutmeg and
   gold leaf, if you like.

Serves 4

Make It Go Further

Before doing your weekly shop, have a good look at the ingredients in your fridge and vegetable rack and think of ways to use them up. You can then go out and buy the ingredients you need to make the most of the items you already have.

Clever leftovers

We all struggle with portion sizing and often have extra rice, potatoes or other ingredients left at the end of each meal. There is a difference between leftovers and waste food. Leftovers are the bits and pieces that sit in a clingfilm-covered bowl in your fridge, challenging you to use them creatively. If you ignore them for four or five days they become waste. Why not try making the most of your leftover bits and bobs?

Ways of using leftovers

There are many ways of using leftover food and slightly over-ripe fruit and vegetables that are starting to wilt. You can:

❑ Simply add the ingredients to a stir-fry, pasta bake, soup, risotto... the list is endless

❑ 'Stretch' the ingredients – sometimes the amount left over is so small it won't go very far in a family setting. Try adding to it. You can cook a little more of it (for example, rice), or try adding lentils and tomatoes to leftover mince to create a whole new take on Bolognese sauce

❑ Make the most of fruit and vegetables that are starting to wilt – use fruit in a crumble, use vegetables in soups and bakes

Alternative suggestions

You may not always feel like transforming your leftovers into meals – or there may not be enough to do so. Another option is to freeze the odd ingredient for later use.

Small amounts of herbs – freeze in ice cube trays

One or two chillies – these freeze well and are easy to chop from frozen

Double cream – lightly whip the cream and then freeze

Cheese – hard cheeses will become crumbly once thawed, but can be used for grating or in cooking

Bread – whiz in a food processor to make breadcrumbs: these freeze well in a sealed plastic bag. Use to sprinkle over bakes for a crisp topping, or to coat fish or chicken before frying, grilling or baking – or use for bread sauce to serve with game or turkey

Leftover Roast Chicken Soup

3 tbsp olive oil, 1 chopped onion, 1 chopped carrot, 2 chopped celery sticks, 2 chopped fresh thyme sprigs, 1 bay leaf, a stripped roast chicken carcass, 150–200g (5–7oz) chopped roast chicken, 200g (7oz) mashed or roast potato, 1 tbsp double cream, salt and freshly ground black pepper.

1 Heat the oil in a large pan. Add the onion, carrot, celery and thyme and fry gently for 20–30 minutes until soft but not brown. Add the bay leaf, chicken carcass and 900ml (1½ pints) boiling water to the pan. Bring to the boil, then reduce the heat and simmer for 5 minutes.

2 Remove the bay leaf and carcass and add the chopped roast chicken and cooked potato to the pan. Simmer for 5 minutes.

3 Whiz the soup in a food processor, pour back into the pan and bring to the boil. Stir in the cream, check the seasoning and serve immediately.

Puddings

Eton Mess

Hands-on time: 10 minutes

200g (7oz) fromage frais, chilled
200g (7oz) low-fat Greek yogurt, chilled
1 tbsp golden caster sugar
2 tbsp strawberry liqueur
6 meringues, roughly crushed
350g (12oz) strawberries, hulled and halved

1 Put the fromage frais and yogurt into a large bowl and stir to combine.
2 Add the sugar, strawberry liqueur, meringues and strawberries. Mix together gently and divide among six serving dishes.

Serves 6

Luscious Lemon Passion Pots

Hands-on time: 5 minutes, plus chilling (optional)

150g (5oz) condensed milk
50ml (2fl oz) double cream
grated zest and juice of 1 large lemon
1 passion fruit

1 Put the condensed milk, double cream and lemon zest and juice into a medium bowl and whisk until thick and fluffy. Spoon into two small ramekins or coffee cups and chill until needed – or carry on with the recipe if you can't wait.

2 To serve, halve the passion fruit, scoop out the seeds and use to decorate the lemon pots.

Serves 2

Perfect Fruit

Most fruits taste marvellous raw, although a few always need to be cooked.
Nearly all fruits make superb desserts when they are baked or poached.

Poaching

To serve four, you will need:
300g (11oz) sugar, 4 ripe pears,
1 lemon, halved.

1 Put the sugar in a large measuring jug and fill with cold water to make 1 litre (1¾ pints). Transfer to a pan and heat gently, stirring now and then, until the sugar has dissolved.
2 Peel and halve the pears, then gently toss with lemon juice.
3 Pour the sugar syrup into a wide-based pan and bring up to a simmer. Put in the pears, cut sides down. They should be completely covered with syrup; add a little more syrup if necessary.
4 Simmer the fruit very gently for 30-40 minutes until the pears are soft when pierced with a knife. Serve hot, warm or cold.

Oven poaching

You can poach fruit in the oven as well. Put the pears in a shallow ovenproof dish and add the syrup as described. Cook at 150°C (130°C fan oven) mark 2 for 30-40 minutes. Under-ripe fruit takes much longer to cook than ripe fruit. Test for doneness regularly, especially in the final stages of cooking. Pears, apples and stone fruits are all well suited to gentle poaching in a sugar syrup.

The secrets to successful poaching are to:
❑ Never let the liquid boil rapidly.
❑ Never overcook the fruit.

Baking

The key to success when baking fruit is in keeping the cooking time short, so that the delicate flesh of the fruit doesn't break down completely. Preheat the oven to 200°C (180°C fan oven) mark 6.

1 Prepare the fruit and put in a single layer in a buttered baking dish or individual dishes. Put a splash of water in the bottom of the dish(es). (For extra flavour, you can use fruit juice or wine instead of water, if you prefer.) Sprinkle the tops with sugar (and other flavourings such as spices, citrus zest or vanilla, if you like). Dot with butter.

2 Bake the fruit until just tender when pierced with a knife or skewer; this should take 15–25 minutes depending on the fruit and the size of the pieces. Leave the fruit to rest for a few minutes before serving.

Good fruits for baking

Fruit	Preparation
Apples (dessert or cooking)	cored and halved or quartered
Apricots	whole or halved and stoned
Bananas	peeled and halved, or in their skins
Berries	whole
Nectarines and peaches	halved and stoned
Pears	cored and halved or quartered
Pineapple	cored and cut into large chunks
Plums	whole or halved and stoned

Poached Plums with Port

Hands-on time: 5 minutes
Cooking time: 20 minutes

75g (3oz) golden caster sugar
2 tbsp port
6 large plums, halved and stoned
1 cinnamon stick
vanilla ice cream to serve (optional)

1 Put the sugar into a pan with 500ml (18fl oz) water. Heat gently until the sugar dissolves. Bring to the boil, reduce the heat and simmer rapidly for 2 minutes without stirring.

2 Stir in the port. Add the plums to the pan with the cinnamon stick and simmer gently for 5–10 minutes until the fruit is tender but still keeping its shape.

3 Remove the plums and put to one side, discarding the cinnamon. Simmer the syrup until it has reduced by two-thirds. Serve the plums warm or cold, drizzled with syrup and with a scoop of vanilla ice cream alongside, if you like.

Serves 4

Baked Apricots with Almonds

Hands-on time: 5 minutes
Cooking time: about 25 minutes

12 apricots, halved and stoned

3 tbsp golden caster sugar

2 tbsp amaretto liqueur

25g (1oz) unsalted butter

25g (1oz) flaked almonds

crème fraîche to serve

1 Preheat the oven to 200°C (180°C fan oven) mark 6. Put the apricot halves, cut side up, into an ovenproof dish. Sprinkle with the sugar, drizzle with the liqueur, then dot each apricot half with a little butter. Scatter the flaked almonds over them.

2 Bake in the oven for 20–25 minutes until the apricots are soft and the juices are syrupy. Serve warm, with crème fraîche.

Serves 6

Quick Apple Tart

Hands-on time: 10 minutes
Cooking time: about 25 minutes

375g pack all-butter ready-rolled
   puff pastry
500g (1lb 2oz) Cox's Orange Pippin
   apples, cored, thinly sliced and
   tossed in the juice of 1 lemon
golden icing sugar to dust

1 Preheat the oven to 200°C (180°C
fan oven) mark 6. Put the pastry on
a 28 × 38cm (11 × 15in) baking sheet
and roll lightly with a rolling pin
to smooth down the pastry. Score
lightly around the edge, to create
a 3cm (1¼in) border.

2 Put the apple slices on top of the
pastry, within the border. Turn the
edge of the pastry halfway over,
so that it reaches the edge of the
apples, then press down and use
your fingers to crimp the edge.
Dust heavily with icing sugar.

3 Bake in the oven for 20–25 minutes
until the pastry is cooked and the
sugar has caramelised. Serve warm,
dusted with more icing sugar.

Serves 8

Strawberry Brûlée

Hands-on time: 15 minutes
Cooking time: 5 minutes, plus cooling and chilling (optional)

250g (9oz) strawberries, hulled
and sliced
2 tsp golden icing sugar
1 vanilla pod
400g (14oz) Greek yogurt
100g (3½oz) golden caster sugar

1 Divide the strawberries among four ramekins and sprinkle with icing sugar.
2 Scrape the seeds from the vanilla pod and stir into the yogurt, then spread the mixture evenly over the strawberries.
3 Preheat the grill to high. Sprinkle the caster sugar evenly over the yogurt until it's well covered.
4 Put the ramekins on a baking sheet or into the grill pan and grill until the sugar turns dark brown and caramelises. Leave for 15 minutes or until the caramel is cool enough to eat, or chill for up to 2 hours before serving.

Serves 4

Summer Fruit Compote

Hands-on time: 10 minutes
Cooking time: 20 minutes, plus cooling and chilling

12 fresh, ripe apricots, halved
  and stoned

125g (4oz) fresh blueberries

50g (2oz) vanilla sugar

juice of 1 orange

200g (7oz) strawberries, hulled
  and halved

Greek yogurt to serve

1 Preheat the oven to 180°C (160°C fan oven) mark 4. Put the apricots, blueberries, sugar and orange juice into a large shallow baking dish and bake, uncovered, for about 20 minutes or until just tender.

2 Gently stir in the strawberries. Taste the cooking juices – you may want to add a little extra sugar – then leave to cool. Cover and chill. Serve with a spoonful of Greek yogurt.

Serves 4

Bread and Butter Pudding

Hands-on time: 10 minutes, plus soaking
Cooking time: about 40 minutes

400g (14oz) panettone, cut into 1cm (½in) slices, then diagonally in half again to make triangles
4 medium eggs
450ml (¾ pint) milk
3 tbsp golden icing sugar

1 Preheat the oven to 180°C (160°C fan oven) mark 4. Arrange the slices of panettone in four 300ml (½ pint) gratin dishes or one 1.2 litre (2 pint) dish.

2 Beat the eggs, milk and 2 tbsp of the sugar in a bowl, and pour over the panettone. Soak for 10 minutes.

3 Put the puddings or pudding in the oven, and bake for 30–40 minutes. Dust with the remaining icing sugar to serve.

Serves 4

Rice Pudding

Hands-on time: 5 minutes
Cooking time: 1½ hours

butter to grease
125g (4oz) short-grain pudding rice
1.1 litres (2 pints) full-fat milk
50g (2oz) golden caster sugar
1 tsp vanilla extract
grated zest of 1 orange (optional)
freshly grated nutmeg to taste

1 Preheat the oven to 170°C (150°C fan oven) mark 3. Lightly butter a 1.7 litre (3 pint) ovenproof dish. Add the rice, milk, sugar, vanilla extract and orange zest, if using, and stir everything together. Grate the nutmeg over the top of the mixture.

2 Bake the pudding in the middle of the oven for 1½ hours or until the top is golden brown, then serve.

Serves 6

Perfect Chocolate

Chocolate is a delicious dessert ingredient. It also makes great decorations, and a simple sauce with many variations. The type of chocolate you choose will have a dramatic effect on the end product. For the best results, buy chocolate that has a high proportion of cocoa solids, preferably at least 70%.

Chocolate shavings

This is the easiest decoration of all because it doesn't call for melting chocolate. Use chilled chocolate.

1 Hold a chocolate bar upright on a worksurface and shave pieces off the edge with a Y-shaped vegetable peeler.
2 Alternatively, grate the chocolate against a coarse or medium-coarse grater to make very fine shavings.

Melting

For cooking or making decorations, chocolate is usually melted first.

1 Break the chocolate into pieces and put in a heatproof bowl or in the top of a double boiler. Set over a pan of gently simmering water.
2 Heat very gently until the chocolate starts to melt, then stir only once or twice until completely melted.

Chocolate curls

1 Spread melted chocolate in a thin layer on a marble slab, baking sheet or clean worksurface. Leave to firm up.
2 Using a sharp, flat-ended blade (such as a metal pastry scraper), push through the chocolate at a 45-degree angle. The size of the curls will be determined by the width of the blade.

Chocolate sauce

1 Chop plain chocolate (at least 70% cocoa solids) and put it in a pan with 50ml (2fl oz) water per 100g (3½oz) chocolate.
2 Heat slowly, allowing the chocolate to melt, then stir until the sauce is smooth.

Rich Chocolate Pots

Hands-on time: 10 minutes, plus chilling
Cooking time: 10 minutes

300g (11oz) plain chocolate (at least
  70% cocoa solids), broken into pieces
300ml (½ pint) double cream
250g (9oz) mascarpone cheese
3 tbsp cognac
1 tbsp vanilla extract
6 tbsp crème fraîche
chocolate curls to decorate
  (see page 167)

1 Melt the plain chocolate in a heatproof bowl set over a pan of gently simmering water. Remove the bowl from the heat and add the cream, mascarpone, cognac and vanilla extract. Mix well – the hot chocolate will melt into the cream and mascarpone.

2 Divide the mixture among six 150ml (¼ pint) glasses and chill for 20 minutes. Spoon some crème fraîche on top of each chocolate pot and decorate with the chocolate curls.

Serves 6

Calorie Gallery

255 cal ♥ 29g protein
13g fat (3g sat) ♥ 2g fibre
7g carb ♥ 0.8g salt

8

215 cal ♥ 16g protein
13g fat (3g sat) ♥ 2g fibre
11g carb ♥ 1.2g salt

10

526cal ♥ 33g protein
29g fat (16g sat) ♥ 4g fibre
34g carb ♥ 4.7g salt

12

(with 1 tbsp low-fat Greek
yogurt): 261 cal ♥ 33g protein
7g fat (2g sat) ♥ 5g fibre
18g carb ♥ 0.5g salt

14

343 cal ♥ 23g protein
28g fat (10g sat) ♥ 1g fibre
0.1g carb ♥ 0.9g salt

30

474 cal ♥ 36g protein
33g fat (9g sat) ♥ 5g fibre
6g carb ♥ 0.6g salt

38

592 cal ♥ 54g protein
18g fat (7g sat) ♥ 6g fibre
56g carb ♥ 1g salt

40

(without cream):
566 cal ♥ 48g protein
12g fat (5g sat) ♥ 3g fibre
71g carb ♥ 1.1g salt

52

540 cal ♥ 35g protein
24g fat (7g sat) ♥ 5g fibre
24g carb ♥ 1.5g salt

54

296 cal ♥ 29g protein
7g fat (1g sat) ♥ 5g fibre
24g carb ♥ 0.4g salt

56

284 cal ♥ 21g protein
17g fat (13g sat) ♥ 2g fibre
11g carb ♥ 0.5g salt

68

266 cal ♥ 24g protein
13g fat (7g sat) ♥ 0.4g fibre
2g carb ♥ 0.9g salt

72

117 cal ♥ 3g protein
6g fat (4g sat) ♥ 4g fibre
13g carb ♥ 0.1g salt

74

519 cal ♥ 33g protein
14g fat (4g sat) ♥ 3g fibre
65g carb ♥ 1.3g salt

80

228 cal ♥ 29g protein
7g fat (1g sat) ♥ 3g fibre
11g carb ♥ 0.5g salt

16

320 cal ♥ 8g protein
24g fat (13g sat) ♥ 6g fibre
18g carb ♥ 1.7g salt

22

399 cal ♥ 17g protein
12g fat (4g sat) ♥ 6g fibre
56g carb ♥ 0.1g salt
24

122 cal ♥ 7g protein
7g fat (1g sat) ♥ 2g fibre
9g carb ♥ 0.3g salt
28

432 cal ♥ 20g protein
20g fat (7g sat) ♥ 5g fibre
46g carb ♥ 1.8g salt

42

490 cal ♥ 39g protein
22g fat (9g sat) ♥ 2g fibre
32g carb ♥ 0.8g salt
44

382 cal ♥ 37g protein
18g fat (6g sat) ♥ 9g fibre
29g carb ♥ 1.2g salt

48

541 cal ♥ 34g protein
25g fat (9g sat) ♥ 6g fibre
30g carb ♥ 1.6g salt
50

217 cal ♥ 13g protein
5g fat (1g sat) ♥ 8g fibre
30g carb ♥ 0.6g salt

58

254 cal ♥ 27g protein
6g fat (1g sat) ♥ 2g fibre
27g carb ♥ 0.9g salt
62

403 cal ♥ 22g protein
17g fat (7g sat) ♥ 5g fibre
40g carb ♥ 1.5g salt

64

267 cal ♥ 16g protein
21g fat (13g sat) ♥ 2g fibre
4g carb ♥ 0.5g salt

66

425 cal ♥ 21g protein
6g fat (1g sat) ♥ 2g fibre
67g carb ♥ 0.9g salt
2

590 cal ♥ 17g protein
19g fat (5g sat) ♥ 3g fibre
81g carb ♥ 2.4g salt

84

339 cal ♥ 6g protein
4g fat (1g sat) ♥ 1g fibre
69g carb ♥ 0.1g salt

86

143 cal ♥ 5g protein
7g fat (1g sat) ♥ 6g fibre
15g carb ♥ 0.1g salt

92

Calorie Gallery

278 cal ♥ 14g protein
22g fat (9g sat) ♥ 7g fibre
7g carb ♥ 2g salt

94

653 cal ♥ 27g protein
24g fat (7g sat) ♥ 10g fibre
83g carb ♥ 1.2g salt

96

440 cal ♥ 19g protein
25g fat (5g sat) ♥ 6g fibre
36g carb ♥ 0.3g salt

98

553 cal ♥ 21g protein
16g fat (2g sat) ♥ 2g fibre
82g carb ♥ 1.3g salt

100

504 cal ♥ 29g protein
24g fat (11g sat) ♥ 8g fibre
45g carb ♥ 2.5g salt

112

416 cal ♥ 47g protein
18g fat (5g sat) ♥ 5g fibre
16g carb ♥ 0.2g salt

120

571 cal ♥ 41g protein
40g fat (22g sat) ♥ 1g fibre
7g carb ♥ 0.2g salt

122

404 cal ♥ 38g protein
12g fat (4g sat) ♥ 12g fibre
40g carb ♥ 1.8g salt

132

392 cal ♥ 33g protein
11g fat (2g sat) ♥ 5g fibre
40g carb ♥ 2g salt

134

317 cal ♥ 25g protein
5g fat (1g sat) ♥ 5g fibre
43g carb ♥ 3.7g salt

136

97 cal ♥ 0.3g protein
0g fat (1g sat) ♥ 1g fibre
23g carb ♥ 0g salt

152

124 cal ♥ 2g protein
6g fat (2g sat) ♥ 2g fibre
16g carb ♥ 0.1g salt

154

202 cal ♥ 3g protein
11g fat (7g sat) ♥ 2g fibre
22g carb ♥ 0.4g salt

156

219 cal ♥ 5g protein
6g fat (4g sat) ♥ 1g fibre
36g carb ♥ 0.4g salt

158

236 cal ♥ 16g protein
17g fat (7g sat) ♥ 3g fibre
6g carb ♥ 0.6g salt

227 cal ♥ 14g protein
4g fat (1g sat) ♥ 15g fibre
33g carb ♥ 1.8g salt

184 cal ♥ 5g protein
11g fat (1g sat) ♥ 9g fibre
18g carb ♥ 1.7g salt

164 cal ♥ 5g protein
8g fat (1g sat) ♥ 9g fibre
22g carb ♥ 2g salt

102

104

106

110

471 cal ♥ 14g protein
29g fat (9g sat) ♥ 6g fibre
38g carb ♥ 3g salt

497 cal ♥ 28g protein
33g fat (13g sat) ♥ 3g fibre
21g carb ♥ 0.4g salt

744 cal ♥ 63g protein
42g fat (18g sat) ♥ 4g fibre
22g carb ♥ 1.6g salt

564 cal ♥ 38g protein
23g fat (11g sat) ♥ 5g fibre
51g carb ♥ 1.6g salt

124

126

128

130

466 cal ♥ 10g protein
31g fat (13g sat) ♥ 1g fibre
41g carb ♥ 1.1g salt

468 cal ♥ 9g protein
20g fat (12g sat) ♥ 1g fibre
62g carb ♥ 1.2g salt

198 cal ♥ 6g protein
5g fat (3g sat) ♥ 1g fibre
33g carb ♥ 0.1g salt

377 cal ♥ 7g protein
21g fat (13g sat) ♥ 0.3g fibre
43g carb ♥ 0.3g salt

138

140

146

148

115 cal ♥ 2g protein
trace fat (0g sat) ♥ 5g fibre
26g carb ♥ trace salt

450 cal ♥ 19g protein
13g fat (5g sat) ♥ 3g fibre
70g carb ♥ 1.1g salt

227 cal ♥ 7g protein
7g fat (5g sat) ♥ 0.1g fibre
33g carb ♥ 0.2g salt

761 cal ♥ 5g protein
67g fat (42g sat) ♥ 2g fibre
31g carb ♥ 0.4g salt

160

162

164

168

Index

PICTURE CREDITS

Photographers: Steve Baxter (pages 31, 43, 63, 83, 87 and 131); Nicki Dowey (pages 25, 39, 51, 59, 95, 97, 99, 133, 135, 155, 159 and 161); Will Heap (page 101); William Lingwood (page 167L); Diane Miller (page 65); Gareth Morgans (pages 15, 29, 57, 67, 69, 81, 85, 103, 111, 113, 121, 123, 127, 137, 139 and 141); Myles New (page 125); Craig Robertson (pages 9, 11, 13, 18, 2, 23, 26, 34, 36, 41, 47, 55, 70, 71, 73, 75, 77, 79, 93, 105, 107, 108, 109, 129, 147, 153, 157, 163, 165, 166, 167R and 169); Maja Smend (pages 45 and 53); Lucinda Symons (page 49); Jon Whitaker (page 17); Kate Whitaker (page 149).

Home Economists:
Anna Burges-Lumsden, Joanna Farros, Emma Jane Frost, Teresa Goldfinch, Alice Hart, Lucy McKelvie, Kim Morphew, Aya Nishimura, Katie Rogers, Bridget Sargeson, Sarah Tildesley, Jennifer White and Mari Mererid Williams.

Stylists:
Susannah Blake, Tamzin Ferdinando, Wei Tang, Sarah Tildesley, Helen Trent and Fanny Ward.

BAKE ME A CAKE

There's always time for cake

EASY PEASY MEALS

Easy meals for every day

LET'S DO BRUNCH

Mouth-watering meals to start your day

CHEAP EATS

Budget-busting ideas that won't break the bank

WONDERFUL ONE-POTS

Easy peasy recipes made in just one pot

Available online at store.anovabooks.com and from all good bookshops

SUPER SOUPS

Sumptuous soups for every day

SKINNY SUPPERS

Delicious, nutritious recipes under 300 calories

SLOW STOPPERS

Slow-cooked meals packed with flavour

GREAT VEG

Inspired ideas for delicious veggie meals

AL FRESCO EATS

Easy grills, barbecues and picnics

ROAST IT

There's nothing better than a delicious roast

FLASH IN THE PAN

Spice up your noodles and stir-fries

GLUTEN-FREE AND EASY

Oh-so-good-for-you recipes that taste great

LOW FAT LOW CAL

Nice recipes don't need to be naughty